The South Pole Ponies

/\

ALEXANDER TURNBULL LIBRARY

The South

Illustrated with photographs and maps

Pole Ponies

THEODORE K. MASON

Introduction by Sir Peter Scott, C.B.E., D.S.C.

DODD, MEAD & COMPANY, NEW YORK

1   2   3   4   5   6   7   8   9   10

Library of Congress Cataloging in Publication Data

Mason, Theodore K
   The South Pole ponies.

   Bibliography: p.
   Includes index.
   SUMMARY: An account of two expeditions, one by
Shackleton, one by Scott, in which Manchurian ponies
were used to help cross the frozen continent in search
of the South Pole.
   1. British Antarctic Expedition, 1907–1909—Juvenile
literature.   2. British Antarctic ("Terra Nova") Expedition, 1910–1913—Juvenile literature.   3. Mongolian
pony—Juvenile literature.   [1. British Antarctic Expedition, 1907–1909.   2. British Antarctic ("Terra Nova")
Expedition, 1910–1913.   3. South Pole.   4. Antarctic
regions.   5. Mongolian pony.   6. Ponies]   I. Title.
G850 1907.B74M37   919.8'9'04   79-52052
ISBN 0-396-07729-3

For Rosemary Casey

ACKNOWLEDGMENTS

The author wishes to thank the following for their kind assistance in gathering material for this book:

The British Library, London

The Cavalry and Guards Club, London

Shirley Cunningham, London

Magda Elias, Elmhurst Branch Librarian, Queensborough Public Library, New York

Joan Fenwick, Kaiapoi, New Zealand

Michael Garside, Cambridge, England

David L. Harrowfield, Antarctic Curator, Canterbury Museum, Christchurch, New Zealand

William Heinemann Ltd., London, publisher of *The Heart of the Antarctic* by Ernest Shackleton

Angela Mathias, Oxted, England, for permission to quote from *The Worst Journey in the World* by Apsley Cherry-Garrard

John Murray Ltd., London, publisher of *Scott's Last Expedition* by Captain R. F. Scott

The New York Public Library

Peter Scott, Cambridge, England

The Scott Polar Research Institute, Cambridge, England

Bridget Lovell-Smith, Photograph Section, Alexander Turnbull Library, Wellington, New Zealand

Joan Woodward, Curator of Pictures, Canterbury Museum

. . . Christopher, who appeared to have come
down to the Antarctic to initiate the well-behaved
inhabitants into all the vices of civilization,
but from beginning to end Oates' management
of this animal might have proved a model to
any governor of a lunatic asylum.

Apsley Cherry-Garrard
The Worst Journey in the World

Contents

Introduction

Although the attainment of the South Pole continues to be one of the most inspiring episodes in the history of exploration, few people today realise the part played in that epic quest by two small bands of unpredictable Manchurian ponies.

The ponies were picked for the historic task after dog teams performed miserably during the *Discovery* Expedition of 1901–1904—my father's pioneering venture in the Antarctic. At that time, little had been seen of the Great White Continent beyond a few coastal sites. No one knew with any certainty what to expect inland or even the best way to get there.

Manchurian ponies had been used to haul supplies on a few expeditions in the Arctic and other northern regions, but the terrain and cold of the Antarctic posed a much greater challenge. The polar route taken by Ernest Shackleton and then by my father's second expedition crossed the world's most awesome ice features, including the Ross Ice Shelf. The surface of this ice barrier—nearly the size of Texas—presented horrendous obstacles to travel, in the form of deep soft snow, hard rippled ice, and hidden crevasses.

As well as exhaustion, hunger, and vitamin deficiency (then unrecognised), the explorers faced the rapidly changing weather conditions which are characteristic of the Antarctic. A glaring sun caused snow-blindness and softened the frozen surface, often making progress agonisingly slow for the marching file of men and beasts. Blizzards brought the column to a halt, sometimes for days. The "chill factor" of the searing winds caused frostbite and cracked and blistered skin.

Using ponies to traverse the Ice Shelf was a daring and innovative plan. Both Shackleton and my father were willing to try out new ideas— an important prerequisite in their initial selection for Antarctic leadership. In addition to the ponies, both of them brought early motor vehicles for crossing the ice. But it was on the hard-working little horses that they placed their highest hopes of bringing up sufficient supplies for the 880-mile trek from McMurdo Sound to the South Pole.

With this book we have the unique opportunity to appreciate the role of the ponies in those historic journeys and the special relationship that developed between them and their handlers. The author, who has been stationed not far from the historic base camps on the Ross Island coast and has visited the South Pole on several occasions, is particularly qualified to tell the story of these splendid little animals.

I have been privileged to go to the Pole for three days myself, to fly over the amazing Beardmore Glacier, and to visit my father's huts at Hut Point and Cape Evans as well as Shackleton's hut at Cape Royds on three separate occasions. I have seen for myself the bales of hay left over in "the stables" at Cape Royds, the rows of bridles at Cape Evans, the special pony snowshoes and all the other equipment. These relics are still in a state of near perfect preservation thanks to the Antarctic cold and the loving care of the New Zealanders from the Canterbury Museum in Christchurch who look after the huts and their contents, and who work each year from New Zealand's Scott Base at the north end of Ross Island.

So it is a special pleasure to be allowed to take part in the launching of this saga of the South Pole ponies.

Peter Scott.

Sir Peter Scott, C.B.E., D.S.C.
The New Grounds,
Gloucester, England

8

PART ONE
Shackleton's Ponies

Horseshoes and comb found on Ross Island

BRITISH ANTARCTIC (*NIMROD*) EXPEDITION, 1907–1909

Shore Party

Ernest Henry Shackleton	Leader
Lieutenant Jameson Adams, Royal Naval Reserve	Meteorologist
Bertram Armytage	General work
Philip Brocklehurst	Assistant geologist
Thomas Edgeworth David	Geologist
Bernard Day	Electrician, mechanic
Ernest Joyce	Stores, dogs manager
Dr. Alister Forbes Mackay	Surgeon
Dr. Eric Marshall	Surgeon, cartographer
George Marston	Artist
Douglas Mawson	Physicist
James Murray	Biologist
Raymond Priestley	Geologist
Williams Roberts	Cook
Frank Wild	Provisions Manager

Others

George Buckley	New Zealand farmer
Alfred Reid	Expedition manager
W. H. Tubman	Pony trainer

Ponies

Billy	Doctor	Mac	Quan	Socks
Chinaman	Grisi	Nimrod	Sandy	Zulu

1 The Wildest Herd of Horse Flesh

THEY sometimes were called "devils" and regarded as being nearly "the wildest herd of horse flesh" ever placed in quarantine. Full of tricks and wickedness, they seemed to be a cross between a pig and a mule and to possess goat-like appetites. They created havoc as well as much needed comic relief on two of the greatest journeys ever made. But despite the problems they caused, these "poor suffering beasts" were highly valued and treated as pets, and every effort was made to keep them alive.

These were the historic Pole ponies. Two English explorers, Ernest Shackleton and Robert Scott, transported these natives of Northern Manchuria to Antarctica to help cross that frozen continent in quest of the South Pole.

It was a daring experiment. The time was the beginning of the twentieth century, when only one continent remained unprobed. Surrounding the South Pole, this area, equivalent to the continental United States and Mexico, offered the last challenge for epic adventure and glory. Of the few who had braved the sentries of icebergs and pack ice in antarctic seas, no one had seen beyond the coast of this unknown land at the bottom of the world. Within the vast continent, two of the world's great geographical prizes, the South Geographic Pole (often called the South Pole or simply the

Pole) and the South Magnetic Pole, beckoned explorers, tempting them like sirens calling from beyond the barren white horizon.

How to reach the poles loomed as the primary problem. Explorers could only guess at what conditions to expect, based on discoveries about frozen wasteland at the other end of the world. Ernest Shackleton was the first to try using ponies to transport his expedition over the ice and snow in 1908. The rugged Irishman had gained polar experience while a member of the pioneering antarctic venture of Robert Scott six years earlier. He had learned firsthand in 1902 the drawbacks of using sledge dogs.

The huskies had had surprising difficulty in pulling sledges on the Ross Ice Shelf, a massive tongue of floating ice permanently attached to the coast. Scott's expedition had to cross this barrier, approximately the size of Texas, on the way to the Pole. Explorers in the Arctic nearly always had used dogs without any significant problems, but in 1902 Scott's dogs had to be shouted at and whipped into making a start. On this, the first attempt on the Pole, the huskies slackened as soon as they heard a voice that was not shouting a sharp command at them, so the men had to abuse the dogs or travel in silence. The dogs at times were intimidated by deep soft snow, on other occasions by low drift blowing in their faces. Their conditions steadily worsened until one by one they were killed to keep the others alive or they died. Without the dogs, the arduous task of pulling supplies became an ordeal that kept the expedition from reaching its goal and nearly cost Shackleton his life.

But Shackleton was determined not to be defeated. He returned to the Antarctic in 1908 as leader of the British Antarctic Expedition, often called the *Nimrod* Expedition. He decided to rely on Manchurian ponies for transportation across the great ice shelf as a result of seeing them himself once in Shanghai and hearing them praised by several knowledgeable people. A friend who had lived in Siberia and Northern Manchuria told Shackleton the ponies were of a peculiarly tough and sturdy stock. He reported that they had done "excellent work in hauling sledges and carrying packs over

12

Postcard issued for Ernest Shackleton's Antarctic Expedition, 1907–1909

snow and ice at very low temperatures and under very severe weather conditions."

Arctic explorers similarly were enthusiastic for pony transport, although the actual performance of the little horses seems questionable. Frederick Jackson took the first ponies to the Arctic on the Jackson-Harmsworth Expedition (1894–1897) to explore Franz Joseph Land, at that time thought to be part of a continent surrounding the North Pole. Jackson acclaimed his four ponies even though they floundered in soft snow up to their bellies and three died.

Albert Armitage, who had served with Jackson as well as with Scott, believed the ponies would fare better than dogs on the level surface of the Ross Ice Shelf. The animals could withstand severe cold and drag a heavier load in proportion to the food they required. Ponies could also provide "better" meat than dogs in case they had to be used as food during the journey.

The impression these reports made on Shackleton is indicated by

13

Alfred Reid, the manager of the *Nimrod* Expedition. Reid told reporters that the ponies could bury themselves up to their noses on their native steppes and could endure temperatures as low as −43° Fahrenheit. Only a "little stubble" was needed to feed them.

In his expedition journal, Shackleton listed the recently concluded Russo-Japanese War (1904–1905) as one of the important reasons for his choice of the ponies over dogs. Manchurian ponies had been used by Russia's fierce Cossack regiments, whose soldiers were fond of fast and reckless riding. Both the Russians and the Japanese used ponies in cavalry units and in pack trains to pull sledges of supplies and field artillery, although the ponies in the pack trains eventually broke down and were replaced by coolies.

The "Boss," as Shackleton was affectionately called by his men, accepted these favorable opinions of the ponies, although they all proved misleading. He was convinced that dogs, the traditional form of polar transport, wouldn't run well on the Ross Ice Shelf, even though dogs used in the Arctic by such explorers as Robert Peary had covered ninety miles a day over level surfaces. Unlike the Arctic, the great ice shelf wasn't a smooth glaciated area. From his experience with Scott's *Discovery* Expedition, Shackleton knew that his venture faced a variety of surface conditions, including deep soft snow, the hard rippled ice called sastrugi, and treacherous crevasses hidden by bridges of frozen snow. The Irishman consequently calculated from all his sources of information that one pony could do the work of at least ten dogs on the same amount of food, in addition to traveling farther in a day's march. One pony could drag a sledge weighing twelve hundred pounds over a broken trail at the rate of twenty to thirty miles a day, he estimated optimistically. The only risk, he thought, was removing the animals from their native climate and shipping them across the tropics and through stormy seas to the Antarctic. But he decided the risk was worth taking and went all-out for the ponies as his primary form of transportation on the journey to the Pole. Only nine dogs and a new Arrol-Johnston motor car were included to assist the ponies on the expedition.

14

A Cossack cavalry unit during the Russo-Japanese War mounted on Manchurian ponies

Through the manager of the London branch of the Hong Kong and Shanghai Bank, Shackleton arranged for a veterinary surgeon in Shanghai to go to Tientsin, China, and select fifteen ponies from a "mob" of about two thousand from the northern regions of China. For some unexplained reason the ponies chosen were all rather old—between twelve and seventeen years. According to Alfred Reid, the ponies were picked by two of the best veterinary surgeons in the Far East. If the press statement of the expedition manager is accurate, the Far East must have been in dire need of a good vet, for the choices were certainly poor ones. Or maybe the men who made the selections were victims of the proverbial horse trader.

Shackleton wrote in his journal that the ponies had lived the early part of their lives in the desolate interior of Manchuria. Some historians believe the first ponies originated in this general area. In time, a few ponies were bred and trained for work by Mongol shepherds, but most were left to run wild and fend for themselves

15

against the elements and packs of wolves. Shackleton's ponies consequently were nearly wild.

The ponies were also big animals, standing about fourteen hands high—a hand equaling four inches. (An equine is formally classified as a pony if it measures less than 14:2 hands at the withers, or shoulders.) Because of the cold climate and lack of feed in their native land, the ponies came from stock that had shortened legs but a powerful body. So they were strong in proportion to their height and surprisingly fast for their size. In fact, they loved to race at unpredictable times, as the antarctic explorers discovered, much to their chagrin.

There were many reasons why ponies were picked over horses for the historic journey. Ponies in general are hardier and easier to keep, and they thrive under conditions that will kill a highly bred horse. Shackleton undoubtedly knew, too, that ponies are patient animals, cheerful and docile if properly treated. They are more intelligent and curious than horses and learn quickly. The drawback is that they learn bad habits as easily as good ones and use their intelligence to take advantage.

The fifteen ponies singled out in China were taken to the coast and shipped by steamer to Australia, while Shackleton and his men left England in a small converted sealing vessel, the *Nimrod*. The Manchurian "mob," as Shackleton later called them, crossed the tropics apparently unscathed by the hot temperatures, arriving in Sydney in late October, 1907. Immediately they were transferred to the *Maheno* and shipped to Port Lyttelton, near the garden city of Christchurch, New Zealand.

When the animals arrived in Lyttelton Harbor on November 8, a *Lyttelton Times* reporter described them as "rough, sturdy-looking fellows . . . with short, thick necks and short heads." Half of them had white coats; all had lost their natural shagginess. Despite the ponies' good qualities, they quickly became known for their tempers. They bit, kicked like mules, and had a "very pretty trick" of hitting with their knees.

From the wharf the ponies were towed in a lighter to Quail

The Manchurian ponies being transferred at Port Lyttleton, New Zealand

Island, 180 acres of grazing land in the harbor, and placed in quarantine there after thirty-five days at sea. During that time the ponies had not been allowed to lie down because experts advised against it. So Quail Island must have seemed like paradise to the poor beasts. As the ponies went ashore, the Lyttelton newspaper reported that they "manifested by various tricks and gambols their natural cussedness and their delight at finding firm earth under hoofs, and green grass within reach of their teeth."

W. H. Tubman holds the reins as two assistants try to manage a fighting Manchurian pony.

Ranging the fields of Quail Island, the herd became sleek and fat until the expedition, without Shackleton, arrived on November 23. The Boss, who was attending to business in Australia, got his first view of them in early December. "They were splendidly strong and healthy, full of tricks and wickedness and ready for any amount of hard work over the snow-fields," he commented. Full of wickedness they proved to be as the job of breaking them in and training them to pull sledges began.

While the *Nimrod* was being strengthened against the ice and loaded with stores, the ponies were turned over to W. H. Tubman, a local horse trainer, and Alistair Mackay of the expedition staff, a Royal Navy surgeon and biologist who had served as a trooper during the Boer War in South Africa (1899–1902). With the ship scheduled to depart in less than a month, the two men had their work cut out for them. More than once they were forced to "make a rapid retreat" from the pony they were handling. Fourteen days before they were housed on the ship, the ponies were still nearly wild. "The little foreigners were quick to show their dislike for human beings and were particularly savage," the local press declared. The white ponies, which later in the Antarctic proved to be the most hardy, were the most difficult to manage.

Although a few people were allowed to visit Quail Island by invitation, the public had to be satisfied with the rather sensational newspaper accounts. A weekly pictorial, the *Canterbury Times*, published photographs to support its claim that the ponies hadn't "proved at all stubborn" and had been "rather apt pupils." A series of pictures illustrated a pony's transformation from breaking in to "serving his master," which meant that a child could ride it or a man could stand on its back. Although the two trainers accomplished amazing results in a very short time, the ponies were far from being tamed.

One of those present during Shackleton's final preparations was W. J. Peters, who had been second-in-command of the 1903–1905 Ziegler Polar Expedition. After seeing the ponies, he said they were very similar to those on the Ziegler enterprise, which "did splendid work toiling faithfully and willingly until they died." It hadn't taken much to feed them, and if Shackleton's animals were half as successful as the Zeigler ponies, Peters claimed, "the task of reaching the South Pole would be robbed of many of its difficulties. On good landlocked ice the ponies could easily drag sledges over 30 miles a day." His remarks must have helped to boost the hopefulness that pervaded the expedition.

During the last of December, Tubman selected for the Boss ten ponies to be used on the journey and devoted all of his attention to them. Zulu was dubbed the leader. Doctor was named after Dr. Mackay; Mac for Aeneas Mackintosh, the second mate; and Nimrod for the ship. Socks's black legs gave him his name. Sandy and Grisi (French for gray) were so-called because of their respective colors. How Chinaman, Billy, and the rascal Quan came by their names was not revealed. One pony that Tubman couldn't control at all he named after Shackleton, who was well known for his fiery temper. The Boss was "much amused," and before sailing he presented the pony to Tubman in recognition of his services. The other four remaining ponies were sold in New Zealand. One of them is known to have lived out its life in the small town of Waikari, about forty miles north of Christchurch.

Food was a prime consideration if the ponies were to be successful on the journey to the Pole. To help feed them in Antarctica, where virtually nothing grows, Shackleton had purchased twenty tons of maize and one thousand pounds of compressed Maujee ration in London. The Maujee ration, a kind of "equine pemmican," was used for feeding horses at Aldershot, one of England's most important military establishments. Consisting of dried beef, carrots, milk, currants, and sugar, it was chosen because it could provide a large amount of nourishment while weighing comparatively little. This was essential if the animals were to pull the loaded sledges a maximum distance every day. The Maujee ration had the additional advantage of being able to absorb water equal to four times its weight, which would further stretch a pony's meal. While in Australia, Shackleton also had purchased ten tons of compressed

W. H. Tubman, aided by members of the Shackleton expedition, breaks in the Manchurian ponies on Quail Island. The New Zealand trainer demonstrated his success by standing on the back of one pony and allowing a child to ride another.

fodder that was made up of oats, bran, and chaff.

On January 1, 1908, the expedition was ready at last to leave Port Lyttelton. After the government veterinary surgeon passed the ten selected ponies, they were ferried from Quail Island to the *Nimrod*. Mac was led into the horse box first and hoisted aboard by twenty sailors using a block and tackle attached to the gaff on the ship's main mast. Tubman coaxed the pony into one of the five stalls that had been built on either side of the forehatch. "In a few minutes the pony was looking interestedly about him, his head hanging peacefully over the padded front rail of his box," according to the *Lyttelton Times*.

One by one the ponies were loaded without incident, which the local press attributed to Tubman's training. Plentiful straw had been provided and mats placed under the animals' feet to help them endure standing up in their narrow stalls during the five-week journey.

Since it was Regatta Day, Lyttelton Harbor was jammed with small boats, and thousands of New Zealanders thronged the shoreline, picnicking and enjoying the warm midsummer weather. (The seasons in the Southern Hemisphere are reversed to those of the Northern Hemisphere.) Strolling near the wharf, impatient crowds waited to have a final look at the *Nimrod*; they were finally allowed to come aboard once the ponies were in position. Expecting to see something like Shetland ponies, the public reportedly was surprised by the large size of the Manchurian breed. But the animals looked "efficient and happy," and to the relief of animal lovers the ponies were "decidedly shaggy," giving them the appearance of being well equipped for the antarctic cold. Either their coats had improved remarkably in a month or this newspaper report was exaggerated.

One of the visitors on that unforgettable morning, George Buckley of Ashburton, couldn't resist the lure of the antarctic adventure. He begged Shackleton, with whom he had become friendly during the expedition's stopover, to let him accompany them as far south as the pack ice. He promised to return on the *Koonya*, a ship chartered to tow the *Nimrod* to the Antarctic Circle so that pre-

George Buckley, the ponies' friend

cious coal needed for fuel could be saved. Shackleton granted permission and Buckley raced into Christchurch to arrange his business affairs. Two hours later, as the *Nimrod* was about to sail, Buckley dashed aboard still wearing his light summer suit and carrying his toothbrush and a change of underwear in a bag tucked under his arm.

A cheering crowd of fifty thousand on the dock gave the expedition a rousing send-off as the *Koonya* led the *Nimrod* through the boat-filled harbor. Weighed down by its heavy load, the *Nimrod* showed only three feet of space between the railing and the water line. Many were pessimistic about the forty-year-old sealing vessel's chances of weathering the stormy seas south of New Zealand, said to be the worst in the world, but Shackleton was confident. By the

23

The Nimrod *is towed from New Zealand toward the Antarctic Circle.*

time the *Nimrod* reached open sea, however, water began to pour through the ports and scupper holes. The leader compared the ship to a reluctant child being dragged to school. Heavy seas soon were washing over the decks, keeping the men continually soaked for two weeks. Lifelines were stretched out and it was risky to move about without hanging onto these ropes.

Shackleton was amazed that the ponies survived the hardships on the trip south. Everything possible was done to care for them, including watches throughout the night with two men in attendance during a shift of two hours. "Inky blackness" pervaded the stalls then, except for a glimmer of light from the salt-encrusted hurricane lamp that jerked about overhead. With each crashing wave the creaking and swaying of the stable roof made it seem ready to collapse. The night watchman often were swept off their feet by seas washing over the forehatch. Yet they cheerfully withstood the bleak and bitter stormy nights in the pony stalls, which they nicknamed the Cavalry Club.

The occupants of the Cavalry Club, however, were far from cheerful about their experience. With frightened whinnies, the ponies fought desperately to stay on their feet in water that flooded the rolling stables. Fierce waves periodically would sweep the deck, tearing the mats from under the ponies' feet and washing the watch keepers almost underneath the struggling animals. During the interludes, the men nailed down the pony mats and then resumed their seats on a bag of fodder fastened to the hatch.

The Boss decided to put the ponies in slings because it was taxing their strength to keep their footing. But when a sling was slipped under one, it nearly went crazy with fright. The animals obviously were only partially broken and still skittish. All the men could do was to try to soothe them with reassuring voices and gentle stroking.

Then to the rescue came George Buckley, the last-minute addition to the trip. Perhaps because he was an experienced farmer, he had a "magical way" with the ponies and they seemed to understand that he was trying to help them. Buckley, whose talents in-

The Nimrod encounters rough seas south of New Zealand.

FROM *The Heart of the Antarctic*

cluded managing sailing boats, also turned his charm on the oppressed ship. When he wasn't in the Cavalry Club, he could be seen on the bridge, coaxing the *Nimrod* through the turbulent seas. "Splendid! Well done, old girl!" he would call out.

On the fifth night from New Zealand, the pony called Doctor slipped during a heavy roll of the ship. When the *Nimrod* rolled the opposite direction, the pony was cast on his back and couldn't get up. The men tried everything in the darkness and rushing water to help Doctor to his feet, but there wasn't enough room to work in the narrow stall. He had to be left on his back with cold seas surging over him throughout the night. The watchmen kept vigil, from time to time giving Doctor handfuls of hay, which he gobbled greedily. Periodically the pony made a frantic effort to gain his feet, but without avail. His struggles became increasingly weaker. When a final attempt to help him up failed the next morning (January 6),

26

Shackleton was forced to have the pony shot to end his suffering.

The men continued to worry about the condition of the remaining ponies. They seemed to be working as hard balancing themselves in their stalls as they would be pulling a sledge all day in the Antarctic. If the ponies went, the men feared their chance of reaching the Pole would be lost, too.

During this rough voyage south, Quan asserted his leadership ability and his cunning, although Zulu had begun the voyage as the head pony. Quan discovered in one of his displays of temper that the soft wood of the stalls could be chewed or given a good battering with his hoofs. Quan then taught this to the other ponies, in the opinion of Professor Edgeworth David, one of the expedition's distinguished geologists. The animals obviously needed some outlet from their torment; under the circumstances, they were patient, courageous creatures. Horses would have thrashed about in their stalls and injured themselves seriously.

The water-soaked men moaned with seasickness as the ocean continued to pour into the ship for a week, smashing part of the starboard bulwarks and the small deckhouse. The Cavalry Club was waterlogged and the men's quarters below were constantly wet. Hand pumps had to be used to help the steam pumps battle the water in the hold and other compartments. To make light of their predicament, the men sang, "Here we go gathering nuts in May."

Fortunately for all on board, there were periodic breaks in the gale. But then the storm would strike again with a vengeance. In the faint light of breaking day on January 11, the *Nimrod* became enveloped in a heavy snow squall. Shackleton suddenly saw the sea rear up alongside the ship. Only the crest of the wave struck, but it had enough force to smash the bulwarks on either side of the Cavalry Club, leaving a free path for the water through the stables. The men no longer had the problem of mucking out the stalls; every swell of the ocean now did the job for them. The herculean wave responsible for the alterations also lifted up one of the whale-boats from its chocks and landed it on top of the stable roof.

The squalls finally gave way to clearer weather and a mackerel

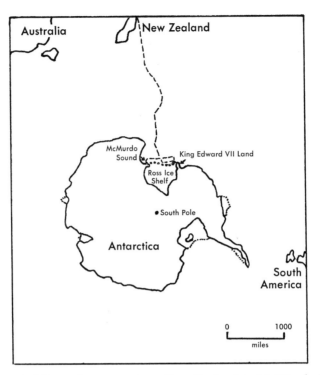

Route of the Nimrod's *voyage from New Zealand to McMurdo Sound*

sky on January 13. In the afternoon one of the dogs, Possum, gave birth to six puppies, adding to the canine population. Using flags, the sailors signaled the news to the *Koonya*, but it took the towing crew a while to understand the transmission. The birth of pups, important to the expedition, was the furthest thing from the towers' thoughts at the time.

In the warm sun on the following day the men began drying their belongings on deck, turning the *Nimrod* into a "veritable Petticoat Lane." A few daring souls took a bath on deck, despite an air temperature of only two degrees above freezing. That evening they all rejoiced with a dinner honoring Buckley, who was credited by everyone with saving the life of at least one pony, Zulu. Most likely he had kept the animal calm and on its feet in the stall despite the rushing water and rolling ship.

The next morning the first iceberg was sighted and the *Koonya* made preparations to depart after having towed the *Nimrod* just over fifteen hundred miles to the Antarctic Circle, an historical event in itself. When a stretch of ice was sighted on the following day, the *Koonya* left with Buckley, the friend of the ponies as well as a man much admired by the expedition.

The Ross Ice Shelf, which the early explorers called the Great Ice Barrier, was sighted a week later. As the crew gawked at one of the world's wonders, the *Nimrod* steamed along its cliff-like edge in search of two inlets discovered previously by Scott and another early explorer. To the dismay of all, the inlets had disappeared. Apparently a great portion of the ice shelf had broken off. In its place was a wide bay filled with ice, penguins, seals, and hundreds of spouting whales. Because of the whales, Shackleton called this place the Bay of Whales, but he quickly decided not to establish his base there. It was obviously too dangerous, since more large chunks of ice might break from the Barrier's face at any time.

Ice chokes the sea along the edge of the Ross Ice Shelf, photographed from 30,000 feet.

MASON

FROM *The Heart of the Antarctic*

Trapped, the Nimrod *waits for a lead to open in the ice pack.*

Despite the danger from the pack ice pressing toward them, the disappointed leader decided to fall back on an earlier plan to set up camp further east at King Edward VII Land. But after several attempts, he was forced to retreat once more. He now had a painful decision to make. Before leaving England he had promised Scott that he would stay away from the McMurdo Sound area, which Scott deemed to be his territory for exploration, based on the trail-blazing of his earlier expedition. Should Shackleton break his promise or give up and return to New Zealand? Being a man of action, he opted for McMurdo. He trusted those in England would understand that the choice was forced upon him by the ice conditions. Unfortunately they didn't. He lost many supporters and became Scott's rival.

2 For a Lick of Salt

THE *Nimrod* sailed around Ross Island and entered McMurdo Sound on January 29, 1908. But the sea ice hadn't broken out yet, preventing the expedition from approaching within twenty miles of Scott's former base at Hut Point, the southernmost promontory of the island. Hoping the ice would break up as it had when he'd been on Scott's *Discovery* Expedition in January of 1902, Shackleton decided to keep the ship in the sound for a few days.

While they waited, Antarctica's animal life put on a spectacular show for the visitors. Comical Adélie penguins lined up on the ice edge and dove into the sea as Weddell seals basked nearby in the warmth of the austral summer sun. The men watched one seal swim under the ice for nearly a quarter of a mile without coming up for air. In the surrounding water, killer whales surfaced, venting air through their blowholes. One occasionally would rise vertically out of the water and peer over the ice edge for a seal dinner. But the most dangerous predators proved to be the Englishmen, who enthusiastically snared penguins, seals, and skua gulls for fresh meat.

On board the *Nimrod*, the crew and shore party prepared to unload so that they would be ready in case the ice moved. They unfastened the beams of the Cavalry Club to permit the ponies a quick exit when the time came. After the 2000-mile voyage, most

FROM *The Heart of the Antarctic*

The men of Shackleton's expedition come to the aid of the broken-down Arrol-Johnston motorcar.

of the ponies were in poor condition, particularly those that were not all white in color. The flanks of nearly all had been skinned by the constant knocking and rubbing against the sides of the stalls. One pony, Nimrod, was such a mass of sores that Shackleton had to have him destroyed. Only eight ponies now remained.

The other forms of transport also were examined during this standoff with the sea ice. Bernard Day, the motor expert, readied the Arrol-Johnston car that Sir William Beardmore, Shackleton's former employer and one of the expedition's primary financial backers, had presented to them. Representing the most modern workmanship, the machine was as much a break with traditional transport as the use of ponies. Day enjoyed such status that it was said the men took off their hats when speaking to him.

On February 1, the experimental car was given a "road" test and became the first machine to move across the antarctic terrain. But the tires unfortunately spun into the soft snow layer and the men had to haul the unsuccessful motorcar back to the ship.

Since the ice refused to budge around Hut Point, Shackleton directed the *Nimrod* north along Ross Island to Cape Royds. The Boss and two companions went ashore and found a small sheltered valley suitable for the expedition's winter quarters. Some of the hardest and most frustrating work to date now began as the ship was unloaded. The car came off first, followed by the dogs, building materials, supplies, and pony fodder. Meanwhile, the carpenter began unbolting the remaining framework of the pony stalls. Sensing their release, the ponies became excited, causing the men a lot of trouble.

In the morning a strong gale buffeted the *Nimrod* against the ice edge, forcing the captain to weigh anchor and steam six miles south to safety. The dogs had to be left tied up on the sea ice alone without shelter or food. When the ship was able to return the next day, the men found that two of the dogs had gotten loose from the picket line and killed over a hundred Adélie penguins, which attracted a mass of skua gulls to a scavenger's feast.

Shackleton lost no time in getting the ponies ashore while the weather was good and the ice remained intact. Disembarking them, however, wasn't a simple matter. The men covered the decks with ashes and padded all sharp objects with bags and bales of fodder. Once a pony was maneuvered into the horse box, the men used the main gaff to sling the box over the side of the ship. The first pony

The first pony is lowered from the Nimrod *to the sea ice of McMurdo Sound.*

CANTERBURY MUSEUM

(unnamed) went in fairly quietly and a few moments later, stamping its feet in the snow layer on the ice, became the pioneer horse in Antarctica. This was on the afternoon of February 5.

One after another the ponies were carefully led out of the stalls and hoisted over the side of the ship onto the ice. Grisi was left until last because he was the most spirited and had come through the ordeal in the best condition. For a few lively minutes Grisi resisted his handlers, but then, at a critical moment, Dr. Mackay applied all of his strength and they managed to get Grisi in the horse box. Grisi, however, wasn't about to give up. He kicked the box violently as he was hoisted up, threatening to demolish the weak structure. When he was finally lowered safely to the ice, Shackleton sighed thankfully.

The ponies immediately began pawing the snow as they had done in Manchuria in wintertime to get at the underlying tussock grass. But here they found only ice.

It was 3:30 A.M. on February 6 by the time all the ponies were unloaded. In the bright sunshine the men carefully led them across a narrow crack in the ice to the shore. The ponies walked very stiffly as a result of their confinement in the stalls, but they all negotiated the fissure safely. The men picketed them on a bare patch of sandy earth at the entrance to a valley about fifty yards from the proposed campsite. This appeared to be an ideal place for the ponies, but soon it would cost the expedition dearly.

Since the Manchurian "mob" was ashore, a party of men had to begin living there, particularly in the event that the *Nimrod* was forced by the weather to retreat out to sea for a time. The rest of the expedition started the arduous job of man-hauling all the supplies across the sea ice to the shore. (In the course of events, the landing site ashore had to be changed to four different locations.)

The ponies were hooked up to the sledges three days later, and began to pull the loads of supplies piled on the ice near the ship to

Right: *The eight surviving ponies of the voyage to Antarctica await their turn at pulling loads of supplies ashore.*

Above: *Dr. Eric Marshall and Bertram Armytage tether a pony to the rope used to anchor the* Nimrod *to the sea ice.*

Chinaman

the shore. Once on shore they had to drag the sledges up steep slopes. But they did their job admirably. With each trip the cracks in the ice began to enlarge so that bridges had to be improvised from the boards of the motorcar case to enable the ponies to cross safely.

On February 11, Dr. Mackay had just arrived on shore with a pony and a loaded sledge while Chinaman and Grisi waited on the ice near the ship for their turn in the harness. Without warning, the greater part of the ice suddenly broke up and began to drift out to sea. Some of the men rushed to the two frightened beasts and quickly guided them off the ice floe nearest the ship and onto the next one, but it too split, stranding Chinaman and Grisi once again. As this was happening, the unsuspecting Mackay started back to the ship with his pony and an empty sledge.

"Don't come any further!" the men on the ship shouted. But the surgeon failed to grasp the situation and continued across the cracking ice. Then a working party at Derrick Point, a high spot of the shoreline, began shouting and waving until he realized what was happening. Leaving his animal, he ran, jumping over the widening fissures to reach the moving chunk with the helpless ponies.

Mackay waited with Chinaman and Grisi as the floe gradually drew closer to a larger piece. When the gap between the floes was only about six inches, he tried to urge Chinaman across, but the pony suddenly became frightened. Rearing up on his hind legs, the poor beast backed up to the opposite edge of the floe and fell into the freezing sea.

Although Mackay hung onto the pony's head rope, it appeared that Chinaman was done for as some of the men who were waiting nearby rushed across the floes to his assistance. While one of the explorers held Grisi, the others managed by pulling and coaxing to get Chinaman's forefeet up on the edge of the ice floe. Then, using all their strength, they managed to lift the distressed animal high enough out of the frigid water to enable him to scramble onto the floe. He stood there wet and trembling, having barely escaped being squeezed to death between the two masses of ice. To warm him up, a bottle of brandy was tossed from the ship and half of it poured down his throat.

The *Nimrod* was turned around and used to push the large ice floe tightly against the fast ice (permanent ice) of the sound. As soon as the crack was closed, the men rushed the ponies across it and took them straight to safety on the shore. How steadily Chinaman, well brandied, crossed the ice isn't recorded. The incident impressed on Shackleton the uncertain nature of the sea ice, and he decided not to risk the ponies on it again.

With perspiration pouring down their faces and bodies, the men worked hard in the hot afternoon sun to move supplies, equipment, and a large quantity of pony fodder to the shore. They finished at midnight. Half an hour later, all of the ice where the provisions had been stacked fell into the sea with a mighty crash. The loss of the scientific equipment would have prohibited a great part of the planned work from being carried out, and the loss of the pony fodder would have meant the loss of the ponies. Even if given a

FROM *The Heart of the Antarctic*

Hauling stores

portion of the men's rations, the ponies couldn't have lasted long.

While a temporary hut and cooking shack were being erected from canvas and bales of fodder, the men labored day and night to unload the remaining stores and coal before the *Nimrod* left to avoid being frozen in the ice. The surrounding surface at the landing site ashore was very rough, yet the ponies didn't seem to be bothered by it at all. They worked as hard as the men at their job of sledging the cases of supplies up from the beach, often in snow or heavy wind. It was a race against the rapidly approaching winter when the sun would not be seen for four cold long months.

On February 18, a four-day blizzard blew the *Nimrod* away from its moorings, and the stores on the shore were buried in frozen salt spray blown a quarter of a mile inland. This first snowstorm quickly changed Shackleton's mind about sheltering the ponies. Originally, he hadn't planned to construct a stable because he had been told by people with the experience of living in Manchuria that the ponies were able to resist cold without protection. But the ponies suffered miserably during the blizzard, particularly because they hadn't fully recovered from the ship journey. Shackleton eventually found that a shelter, even one not warmed to a high temperature,

38

would keep the ponies in better condition than if they were allowed to stand in the open.

During the storm the shore party had taken refuge in the main hut, but it provided little warmth because the insulation and other aspects of the construction weren't finished yet. More of the men began living in the structure on February 22 following the blizzard when the *Nimrod* departed for New Zealand and the job of moving the landed provisions closer to the hut continued.

The hut was built from yellow pine with a four-inch layer of cork between the sheathings and sunk into a foundation of cement mixed at the site. Measuring 33 by 19 feet, it was situated about 120 feet above the sea on the slopes leading to smoking Mount Erebus. Like the keep of a castle, the snow-blanketed volcano dominated the white landscape. Adélie penguins had established one of their large, smelly rookeries on the rocky beach a few hundred yards away from the hut. To the north, a number of small, frozen lakes added scientific and aesthetic interest as well as providing an exercise area for the ponies during the winter.

The fourteen men under Shackleton's command were assigned floor space in the hut by pairs, about six feet, six inches for two men.

Shackleton's winter quarters at Cape Royds, as it appears today, situated a short distance from frozen Pony Lake

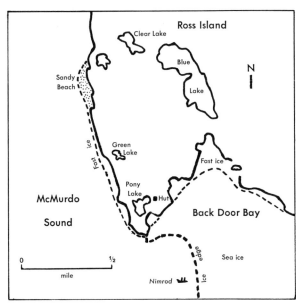

Map of Cape Royds

They used planks and broken up boxes to construct bunks and hung canvas to curtain off the two-man cubicles. Only Shackleton's tiny room was partitioned with boards. After some initial trouble with the stove, the crowded hut was completed and the acetylene lamp lit for the first time on March 3.

A nose bag and feed box hang from the remaining beam of the pony stables at Cape Royds.

The lee side of the hut subsequently became the inside wall of the stables where the ponies would be housed during the forthcoming winter. The outside wall was made with bales of fodder. To close one end, a double row of cases of maize were stacked five feet, eight inches high. A doorway was left at the opposite end, with a wide plank cemented into the ground.

A canvas tarpaulin was pulled over the top for the roof; planks and battens were added on both sides to support the tarpaulin during storms. Finally, a wire rope was stretched along the inside wall to tie the ponies' head ropes.

The ponies, however, weren't as impressed with their quarters as the builders were. During the first night the animals spent in the new stables no one got much sleep. Some of the ponies broke loose and trotted a short distance away. The exhausted men had to scramble out of their bunks and fetch them back. Once calm was restored, the devilish Grisi went into action. He pushed his head into the hut through one of the half-boarded windows and woke the expedition with a resounding whinny. The muttering men were forced to board up the top halves of the hut windows along the common wall with the stable.

Later, the first strong wind shook the roof of the stable so much that the men feared it would blow away. After the gale, all the spare sledges were laid on top of the stable and tied down with stout rope. The next snowfall blanketed the sledges, making a perfect, wind-sturdy roof.

With the construction completed, there was time to turn to other projects. Shackleton had planned for two sledging journeys before the winter set in, but they had to be abandoned because the sea ice had broken up in the sound. With it went the only sledging route.

The energetic Edgeworth David was full of ideas for worthy projects, however. He suggested that a party undertake the first ascent of Mount Erebus and make various scientific observations. The Boss approved, and on March 5 David set off with five companions to begin the historic climb. They returned on March 11 to find that disaster had struck the base. The pony Sandy had become

George Marston inspects picketed ponies at Cape Royds.

mysteriously ill and died. Dr. Eric Marshall, one of the surgeons, performed a postmortem and found the pony's stomach to be full of volcanic sand.

Quickly the ponies were shifted from Sandy Beach where they were picketed and moved to a shelter on the lee side of the hut. They were given treatment, but it was too late. At midnight on March 12, Raymond Priestley found Billy down in his stall. Despite all efforts, the men couldn't get him on his feet and he died on the thirteenth. Zulu followed. Mac began to falter on March 14 and had to be shot the next day. A postmortem revealed, however, that

42

he had died of corrosive poisoning as the result of eating wood shavings that had been used to pack chemicals in one of the cases. Shackleton blamed the "breed's goat-like craving" to eat anything that could be chewed. He blamed himself, however, for not giving the ponies their needed supply of salt. Apparently the ponies, having been picketed on sandy ground when the expedition first landed, had discovered a saline flavor in the volcanic sand as a result of salt spray from the sea. The site of the winter quarters, which at first seemed so promising, had cost the expedition dearly indeed.

David placed much of the responsibility on Quan, undoubtedly because of the pony's leadership in the attack on the shipboard stalls during the voyage south. According to David, Quan had developed a taste for eating fragments of felspar crystals, combined with chips of lava. These he "strongly recommended to the other ponies, four of whom followed his advice, and in a few hours all five were converted into walking geological museums."

Quan, the ringleader, survived, and the expedition was left with only four ponies; Quan, Socks, Grisi, and Chinaman. Curiously, the survivors were the light-colored ponies, the darker-colored ones all having met with disaster. This was the second occasion on which the white ponies fared better, confirming the belief that they were more hardy.

The deaths were a serious blow to the expedition because Shackleton had considered six ponies the minimum requirement for his trek to the Pole. The remaining ponies consequently were regarded as very precious and watched carefully. The dogs became more important as well. Although only eight had survived the trip south, a number of births had brought the total to twenty-two. All had to be trained to pull the sledges. The new pups were to become an unsuspected bonus to the expedition.

3 Winter Preparations

As the long winter night crept stealthily toward them, the men were kept busy with house chores, preparing equipment, recording a variety of scientific observations, and producing the first antarctic book on a printing press they had brought with them. For recreation they had books to read and such games as chess and dominoes. They also had the animals to care for, which took considerable time and effort.

The remaining four ponies were exercised by walking. Before the daylight grew faint, the usual morning walk was over the hills along the coast to Sandy Beach, where the ponies had a roll on the soft volcanic sand but no time to eat. Then a circuit was made around Blue Lake and Back Door Bay to the hut. Sometimes for a change the ponies were taken to the snow slopes and foothills of Mount Erebus behind the hut. The men rode the ponies on level stretches until the fading light caused fears that the animals might stumble.

In April, the sun began to disappear below the horizon, shortening each day until the twenty-third, when it sank behind the coastal mountains in a blaze of golden glory. After two weeks of twilight, the continual darkness of the antarctic winter clamped down on the little hut at Cape Royds, except for the light from the stars and

Shackleton's hut at Cape Royds in winter, with stables adjacent to the right wall

moon on clear nights. The fifteen explorers and their animals were completely isolated on the vast, hostile continent, thousands of miles from civilization.

Now that it was too dark to cross the rough ground safely, the ponies were taken up and down the snow-covered lake called Green Park close to the hut. The men who usually took the ponies for exercise soon learned their individual traits. In common the ponies all seemed to possess more cunning and sense than the English horses the men were accustomed to handling. The worst offender of course was Quan, who raised hell inside the stables. He took delight in biting through his head rope and attacking the bales of fodder stacked behind him. When a chain was put on him to stop this, the Manchurian monster "deliberately" rattled it against the side of the hut, keeping everyone awake.

Quan also liked to take the wire rope to which the ponies were tied and, pulling it back as far as possible, let it go with a bang against the galvanized iron wall of the hut. The men tried to stop him by keeping his nose bag on, but within a few hours he ate a

45

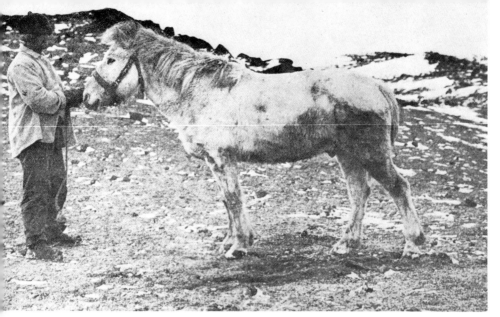

FROM *The Heart of the Antarctic*

Quan, the "delinquent"

hole through the bag and began banging the rope once more. Again, everyone was wide awake.

Fortunately for Quan, the men couldn't remain annoyed at him for long. On going to the stables to stop the "delinquent's" mischief, they were impressed by the intelligent look on his face as he rolled his eye and leered as though to say, "Ha! Got the best of you again." But their sporting sense of humor had been tested far enough. They tethered all four legs and peace reigned in the stables, at least temporarily.

Quan surprisingly was the general favorite among the ponies despite his chain rattling early in the winter and the "ugly" appearance that Shackleton described as "great raw-boned." He continued to be a sand addict and had to be watched carefully when being exercised. If his handler was momentarily distracted, Quan would immediately start crunching a mouthful of the loose volcanic material exposed in patches on the Ross Island slopes. Undoubtedly Quan, or "old Quan" as he was often called, provided a welcome diversion from the stress of the rigorous living conditions. Although he was a prankster, Quan was better natured than the other ponies, which the men appreciatively noted when leading him on a walk.

FROM *The Heart of the Antarctic*

The spirited Grisi

Grisi, the most spirited of the ponies, was thought to be the best looking. He was dappled with gray and moved in a "very pretty" way. But his conduct in the stables was far from attractive. He was temperamental and aggressive toward the other ponies. On the slightest provocation he would lash out with his powerful hind feet. He became nervous and high strung during the dark winter months, even though the men built him a separate stall in the far corner and kept a lamp continually burning in the stables.

Also described as a pretty little pony, Socks was shaped some-

Socks earned his name because of the feather-like hairs on the backs of his legs.

FROM *The Heart of the Antarctic*

FROM *The Heart of the Antarctic*

A night watchman reads next to the hut stove while listening for any disturbance in the stables.

thing like a small Clydesdale with feather-like hairs on the backs of his legs. Socks displayed an eagerness to work, but his handlers had to beware of his fiery temperament.

The remaining pony, the strong Chinaman, was sulky in appearance, but Shackleton considered him to be one of the best of the lot. He had a habit of chewing through his head rope, which was cured by replacing the rope with a chain.

During the first part of the winter, a night watch was established to look after the hut while the others slept. One of the night watchman's duties was to listen for any suspicious noises from the stables and, regardless of how quiet they were, to inspect the animals every two hours. During the day the ponies were looked after by Bertram Armytage and Dr. Mackay, until midwinter when Armytage took over. An Australian assigned to general duties, Armytage was the member of the expedition most willing to get up at 7:30 A.M. when the last night watchman retired. Perhaps he felt it was his duty since, unlike the others, he wasn't a specialist.

After a few months, the night watchman no longer had to make his two-hourly rounds of the stables, thanks to the "little army" of pups whelped by the expedition's five bitches by midwinter. During the cold weather the puppies slept in the stables instead of outdoors with the other dogs. If a pony managed to get loose, the pups would surround him, barking furiously until the night watchman arrived.

The pups showed their worth on a number of occasions. One night Grisi got free and dashed out of the stables. All of the pups followed the pony and managed to round him up on the frozen Green Park Lake. Dr. Mackay ran to retrieve the truant. As he led Grisi back to the stables, the pups followed with "an air of pride as though conscious of having done their duty."

By the end of the winter, Shackleton had enough dogs for a large sledge team. The huskies responded surprisingly well to pulling the sledge during training, although some, such as Scamp, were a problem. Scamp had been used as a sheep dog in New Zealand, and when he was taken for a walk with the other dogs was always trying to round them up as if they were sheep. Shackleton believed the other dogs enjoyed their walks much more when Scamp was absent.

A series of short sledge journeys in mid-August gave the dogs and most of the men their first experience of polar field work under cold conditions. Shackleton, accompanied by David and Armytage,

George Marston's watercolor depicts several of Shackleton's men walking with dogs during the Antarctic winter darkness. Overhead, the Aurora Australis snakes its way across the sky.

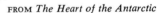

FROM *The Heart of the Antarctic*

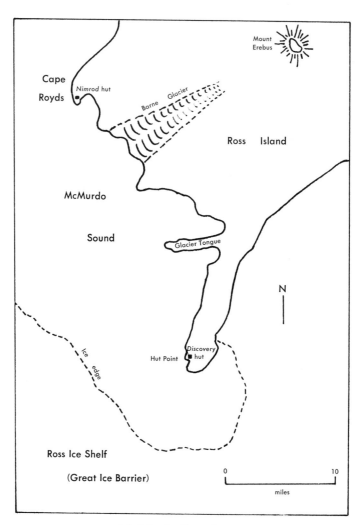

McMurdo Sound area

made the first, a 23-mile trip on August 12 to Scott's *Discovery* Expedition quarters at Hut Point. Old Quan was picked to pull their sledge of supplies, perhaps because he often had so much excess energy. But the march proved too difficult and Quan was sent back after an hour. Temperatures were still low (−56° F.) and the weather unpredictable (a five-day blizzard trapped them at Hut Point).

50

After suffering indigestion from the "hoosh" (a kind of stew fixed at most meals), frozen beards and moustaches, and wet sleeping bags, the group was delighted to get back to the "civilization" of winter quarters on August 22. The expedition happily enjoyed its first glimpse of the returning light that day as well, although the sun didn't appear fully until early September.

During September, the Boss began sending similar small parties to Hut Point every week for more sledging practice and to transfer supplies there for eventual use on the journey to the Pole. On the twenty-second, Shackleton and five companions left Cape Royds to establish a cache of oil and pony maize on the Ross Ice Shelf. The car gave them a lift for the first eight miles; then they continued on, each man hauling a 168-pound sledge. It took the depot-laying party two weeks, in severe weather with temperatures plummeting to −59° F., to reach their goal, 138 statute miles from Cape Royds. Called Depot A, the cache of four days' food for the ponies on the trip to the Pole was marked by an upturned sledge and a black flag on a bamboo pole.

The depot-laying party returned to base on October 13, arriving after the Northern Party, led by David, had departed on October 5, man-hauling sledges, to the South Magnetic Pole. (At that time, the South Magnetic Pole was situated about four hundred miles north of Cape Royds and twelve hundred miles north of the South Geographic Pole, the goal of Shackleton's Southern Party.)

Quan, Socks, Chinaman, and Grisi (left to right) *with handlers before departing Cape Royds*

Instead of making a string of depots along the route to the Pole, the Boss decided to rely on the ponies to haul enough supplies with them on the journey. In addition, a supporting party with the motorcar would help transport the supplies during the initial stage of the trip, which turned out to be for only twenty miles south of Hut Point. Everything needed had to be stored on the ice shelf in advance or taken with them. There were no airplanes at that time or other means of reaching the Southern Party once it was underway across the barren wastes.

During this period while the men were training and gaining experience, the ponies were being exercised regularly along the sea ice from the winter quarters to Cape Barne, about three miles. Shackleton felt the little horses would justify his confidence in them, but he was anxious that they shouldn't be overloaded, thereby reducing their speed. If the 1776-mile trek to the Pole and back to Hut Point were to succeed, the ponies couldn't be overworked in the early stages of the journey across the ice shelf. So the Boss began trying loads of varying weights and determined that the maximum the ponies could haul efficiently was 650 pounds each, including a 60-pound sledge. This capacity was only half of the 1200-pound load he had originally calculated that the ponies could manage, based on the reports of their previous work. Some adjustments could be made but, with the loss of four ponies during the early part of the winter, Shackleton had to cut back severely on the amount of food that he could take on the march to the Pole.

There were other preparations to ensure the welfare of the remaining four ponies. The harness for each was designed with a broad leather band around the chest, to which traces made of alpine rope were attached. The traces in turn were toggled to a whiffletree, or crossbar, which was fixed to the center of the sledge bow. There was also a strap over the neck of the pony to support the hauling band and a strap across the back with a girth around the belly. Great care was taken to keep the harness free from ice and dirt so that it wouldn't chafe the pony when it sweated and the moisture condensed into ice from the cold. Finally, all the buckles

*Pony harness used by Ernest
Shackleton's expedition*
D. L. HARROWFIELD,
CANTERBURY MUSEUM

were leather-covered in order that no cold metal would touch the pony.

Of those who had gained the most sledging experience, Shackleton picked the three men best medically fit to accompany him on the polar odyssey. Jameson Boyd Adams, a meteorologist, was appointed second-in-command, even though at twenty-eight he was the youngest member of the expedition. Before joining the venture, Adams had spent three years as a lieutenant in the Royal Naval Reserve. Dr. Marshall, twenty-nine, had been a football player before qualifying as a surgeon. Frank Wild at thirty-five was the oldest. A direct descendant of Captain James Cook who first sailed around the continent, Wild as well as Shackleton had been on Scott's *Discovery* Expedition. The Boss was a year younger than Wild.

53

FROM *The Heart of the Antarctic*

Guiding ponies along the cliffs of Ross Island and down to the sea ice to begin the Southern Journey

Shackleton had high expectations for the success of the Southern Party, even though Quan had been lame for a week before it started for Hut Point. The pony had been doctored and Shackleton believed the problem had been licked. Lameness in such old ponies, however, is often a recurring malady.

The Boss continued to be optimistic, especially after seeing what he considered a good omen during the party's last dinner together at Cape Royds. As they were sitting at the table, the evening sun entered through the ventilator and shone a circle of light on the picture of Queen Alexandra. Slowly it moved across the wall and lit up the photograph of King Edward VII. Only on that day and at that particular time could it have happened, just hours before they were to begin their quest to plant the English flag on the "last" unexplored spot on earth.

The next morning, October 29, 1908, they began the transit from Cape Royds to Hut Point over the sea ice near the shore of the island. Overland, the mountainous terrain was too rugged and crevassed for safe traveling, especially for ponies. The sea route had to be used before the ice broke up in late spring. It also had a roadblock in the form of Glacier Tongue, the crevassed tip of a glacier jutting five miles out into McMurdo Sound from Ross Island.

A six-man supporting party with the motorcar towing two sledge loads started first at nine-thirty; half an hour later, the Boss' Southern Party followed, leading the ponies with empty sledges. Only two men, including the cook, were left behind.

To make it easier for the ponies, the car was to pull the supplies as far as possible. The dogs were kept in reserve. They were to be used by Ernest Joyce and a small party to lay a depot off Minna Bluff, about eighty-five miles from Hut Point, during January and to add more supplies in February. Shackleton instructed Joyce to wait with his men and dogs at this storage site, called Bluff Depot, until February 10 to meet the Southern Party returning from the Pole.

When the Southern Party said its good-byes, the men paused silently with clasped hands. Then they made their start, turning momentarily to acknowledge a cheer from the two lonely figures standing on the ice by the familiar cliffs of Cape Royds.

Any feeling of enthusiasm was squelched only an hour later when the hard-working Socks abruptly went lame, most likely from injurying himself on a piece of sharp ice. It was particularly depressing after Quan's recent lameness. Although the party was forced to continue on to Hut Point, Shackleton decided he would not leave Scott's former base until Socks recovered. He had no other choice. Their food supply had been calculated to the ounce, and all the ponies were needed to transport it.

They camped at one o'clock and fed the ponies before sitting down on the sledge to eat near their steeds. Without warning, Grisi had one of his unexplainable kicking tantrums and struck Adams just below the knee. A few inches higher and Adams would have been incapacitated with a shattered knee cap. As it was, the bone was nearly exposed in his leg. Despite the pain, Adams said very little about it and the party continued after lunch.

In the early afternoon they caught up with the support party and the car, which had been prevented from going farther by pressure ridges and drifts around Glacier Tongue. Since it was obvious the experimental vehicle would never make it very far across the Barrier, Shackleton sent Day and two helpers back to Cape Royds with the car. The Southern Party moved on to the south side of Glacier Tongue, where they spent four hard hours grinding six hundred pounds of maize to feed the ponies on the journey. At nine o'clock in the evening, they cooked a hoosh, while a warm sun beat down on them from a brilliantly clear sky. Mount Erebus behind them blasted three distinct columns of steam into the cold air over Ross Island.

The ponies were quiet except for Quan who decided to try one of his old tricks: biting his tether. Observing the prankster, Shackleton thought, "If this goes on, I'll have to send for a wire rope." But during the night, Shackleton found Quan out. A wind had begun to blow, causing drifting snow. From time to time the leader peeked out of the tent to check on the ponies. He soon discovered that Quan continued biting his tether only as long as he thought someone was watching him. As soon as the Boss closed the tent flap, he promptly stopped.

When Shackleton's group reached Hut Point the next afternoon, both Adams and Socks seemed to be better, much to everyone's relief. Two hours later, the support party caught up with them and camped outside the old hut in a tent.

The weather was snowy and dull during the next few days while the men did various chores and some geological work in the nearby hills. Shackleton, Dr. Marshall, and Armytage returned with the three uninjured ponies to Glacier Tongue to pick up some pony food left behind. The animals pulled admirably when they were hitched to 500-pound loads, despite poor light and a rough surface. Grisi kept things lively by bolting off with his sledge, but luckily he didn't run far. The heavily laden sledge undoubtedly played an

FROM *The Heart of the Antarctic*

Shackleton's party camped on the sea ice near Hut Point. Robert Scott's Discovery *hut can be seen in the background, upper left.*

important part in his decision to stop.

A day later, November 1, the expedition was together again at Hut Point, packing for the actual start of the trip to the Pole. They were temporarily held up by Socks, whose foot was "seriously out of order." It was almost a disaster, for "we want every pound of hauling power," Shackleton worried. Eventually, Socks was to become the pony that decided the fate of the expedition.

The next morning when the men woke, they found that Quan had bitten through his tether and played havoc with the maize and fodder, as though angered that no one paid any attention to his tether-eating game. As soon as he saw Shackleton coming down to where the ponies were picketed, he started dashing from one sledge to the next, tearing the bags to pieces and trampling the food. Only one sledge of fodder remained untouched ten minutes later when the men finally caught the delinquent. Quan then pranced around, kicking up his heels as if to demonstrate that the incident had been a deliberate piece of destructiveness. He had eaten his fill of many pounds of maize before the rampage, evidenced by his bulging belly.

In the afternoon Quan, Grisi, and Chinaman pulled sledges a few

57

Holding Quan, the Boss inspects ponies on the picket line.

miles to the junction of the sea ice and the permanent ice shelf. They made commendable progress despite the soft snow. The sun was blazing gloriously and the wind had dropped, indicating fine weather for the next day's departure as they returned to Hut Point. At the same time, Socks seemed much better and Adams' leg was nearly well. Everything appeared encouraging. Shackleton had one primary concern: that the ponies continue pulling well for at least a month.

4 Toward the White Nothingness

FLAGS flying from poles on the sledges, Shackleton's Southern Party left Hut Point on November 3, the real start of the 1776-mile journey to the Pole. (Distances represent statute miles in a straight line, not the actual miles covered by the explorers who at times had to travel up and down ice ridges and make detours.)

The four ponies each pulled a load of 600 pounds or more. Quan, as was to become customary, pulled the heaviest: 660 pounds. A supporting party of five men together hauled the same load as Quan, and this included 153 pounds of pony feed. The support group was to return in five days, after their contribution was cached on the ice shelf, or Barrier.

Shackleton planned to give each pony ten pounds of food per day, and in all nine hundred pounds were taken for the animals. Although the Boss didn't emphasize it, there was only enough to feed the ponies for twenty-five days. The men, on the other hand, were to be allowed thirty-four ounces each per day, enough for 91 days or, if they could stretch the rations, as much as 120 days. From these calculations it is obvious that Shackleton intended to take the ponies no farther than across the four hundred miles of permanent ice shelf, which began about five miles beyond Hut Point.

Soon after they got underway, the expedition found that due to the hot sun the snow on the frozen sound near Hut Point was so soft that the ponies continually sank up to their hocks and sometimes up to their bellies. The party left the ice-covered sea about an hour later, after joining up with the supporting party, and started over the Barrier. To their surprise, the snow surface on the Barrier was even softer. The ponies, however, pulled magnificently, with the support party "toiling painfully in their wake." If anyone viewed this beginning as an indication of possible trouble with the surface during the journey, he didn't mention it.

At one o'clock the advance group pitched camp, tethered the ponies, and lunched on tea with plasmon (a kind of protoplasm preparation), plasmon biscuits, and cheese. Afterward, the supporting party pushed on while the pony handlers did the camp work. When they finished and started off, they found the surface crust hard enough to support the weight of a man, but the ponies had to plow through it as before. The ponies also had another problem to deal with. Their "weather sides" remained dry while their lee sides were frosted with condensed sweat. In such misery they plodded on. The supporting party and the Southern Party itself took turns man-hauling the sledges, but even with this help it was obvious that the men couldn't keep up with the ponies.

When they camped for the evening after covering twelve miles, the men fed the ponies and had dinner. The meal was followed by "the most ideal smoke a man could wish for after a day's sledging," even though the men's lips were already beginning to crack from the dry, cold air and the hot metal pans they ate from. After their dinner, they gave the "gallant, little ponies" some biscuits to eat since there were plenty to spare. The ponies stood comfortably in the sun with the temperature at 14° F., a mild day under antarctic conditions. Occasionally they pawed the snow, and the energetic Grisi eventually dug a large hole in the soft surface.

The men wore goggles the following day when the two groups started, after depositing one hundred pounds of oil and provisions for the return journey. They needed the goggles to protect their

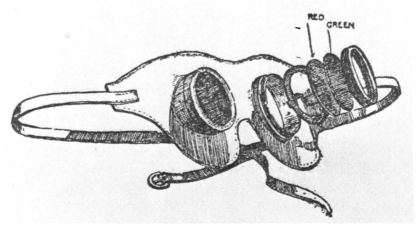

Snow goggles worn by the Southern Party

eyes from the bright glare of the sun and ice, which can cause a temporary blindness. The ponies, however, had to make do without. After a good start the surface became softer in the afternoon, and by the time the expedition stopped in the evening both ponies and men were exhausted from pulling their loads through the snow.

Falling snow on the next day (November 5) added a new thick coating to the surface, compounding the ordeal for man and beast. The light was so poor that it was difficult to see the patches of sastrugi, often slippery and sharp. Suddenly Dr. Marshall and Grisi stepped into a crevasse. The sledge luckily caught on the snow-bridge that often crosses such chasms. Scrambling out of the crack in the ice, Marshall shouted the danger to the others and helped Grisi out. When Shackleton inspected the opening, the first of the journey, he found it about three feet across, with sides widening out below and no discernible bottom.

Shackleton quickly altered their course, but in fifteen minutes Wild, Adams, and Marshall were momentarily trapped in a narrow crevasse. Although they escaped easily, the leader ordered a halt. The party pitched camp in the middle of this field of hazards to wait for the weather to clear. But a blizzard began to blow hard, and the

FROM *The Heart of the Antarctic*

George Marston's painting of the Southern Party camped in a blizzard on the Ross Ice Shelf

men were forced to spend the following day in their sleeping bags reading. They emerged only to feed the ponies, which they could barely see through the peepholes in their tents.

The storm was their first setback of the journey, and many of the men didn't eat for twenty-four hours to conserve the food that was so scrupulously rationed. Standing with their tails to the wind, the ponies, however, had to be fed their full forty-pound ration. Quan and Chinaman gobbled up theirs, but Socks and Grisi didn't eat so well. They all preferred the Maujee ration and ate that before the ground maize.

Next morning, November 7, the men assembled after scraping the snow off their sledges and tents. In front of them appeared a "dead white wall" with nothing, not even the shape of a cloud, to guide them. But regardless of the ominous horizon, it was time for the support party to return, after traveling thirty-eight miles from Hut Point. The six men gave Shackleton and his companions three cheers as the Southern Party struck out toward the white nothingness; then they headed back to Ross Island.

The ponies started pulling well, but within a half-mile they began to break through the crust, discovering a maze of crevasses. The first chasm Dr. Marshall and Grisi crossed was six feet wide with a "black yawning void" below. Shackleton stopped Quan on what he thought was the side of one, but in the dim light he couldn't be certain. Taking a closer look, he discovered that they already were standing on the snowbridge crossing the middle of the crevice. Gingerly, Shackleton unharnessed Quan from the sledge and eased the spirited pony along the frozen span to safety. The sledge with their three months' provisions was next rescued from plunging into a bottomless brink. Then Adams crossed another crevasse, and Chinaman put his foot into the side of it. Shackleton, following with

MASON

Crevasses

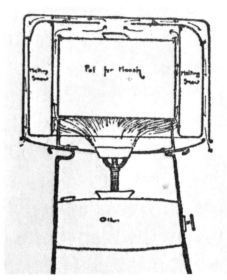

Type of cooker used by Shackleton's expedition and other early explorers

FROM *The Heart of the Antarctic*

Quan, also got into trouble. That was enough! Shackleton called a halt and they pitched their two tents. Less than a mile had been traversed that day.

They were forced to spend the following day (November 8) in their sleeping bags while outside their tents the wind whirled new snow around them. They lay there impatiently all day, watching the drifting on the sides of the tent. Time, which meant irreplaceable food, was being lost as if blown away by the wind. When they fed the ponies, the men found that Socks and Grisi still weren't eating well. The hard maize didn't seem to agree with them. So at lunch the men used precious oil to boil some Maujee ration to give the ponies a hot hoosh, which they ate readily. It seemed to perk them up after they had been standing for most of four days in drifted snow.

In the evening the weather cleared, revealing the horizon but also a "nest of crevasses" around them. Two of the men discovered they had pitched their tent right on the edge of one. Yet despite

64

their precarious position, they turned in and went to sleep.

When the party woke the next day, the weather was clear and calm. They all set to work using their ice axes to probe a track through the concealed crevasse field. The openings they found varied from small cracks to gaping gulfs. One they tested by dropping a chunk of frozen snow into it. Hearing no sound, they decided the bottom was far below.

The ponies, which had become stiff during the blizzard, weren't pulling very well when the party finally got underway. They made it safely over the first crevasses, but then Chinaman stepped into the side of one. Adams struggled to keep the pony from going in farther as Shackleton and Wild ran to help. Carefully they coaxed the frightened pony to step back until he was extricated from the potential disaster. Inspecting the three-foot crack, the men found it opened into a great chasm, in which they would have lost Chinaman, all their cooking gear, biscuits, half of the oil, and probably Adams as well. Chinaman by this stage must have had serious doubts about the whole enterprise. After weathering the voyage south, the poor pony had narrowly escaped being lost on several occasions, first in the freezing sea and then in an assortment of crevasses.

As though the Antarctic had tested them enough, the party encountered no more crevasses in that area and made good progress on an improving surface. The men camped at six o'clock and boiled more Maujee ration for the ponies; it smelled so good, in fact, that the explorers were tempted to try it. After dinner, Quan began his game of gnawing his tether rope. Shackleton tried securing him by the hind leg, but Quan discovered that by lifting this leg he could reach the rope and continue munching away at it. The Boss finally put a stop to the nonsense by slipping a nose bag on his delinquent.

The men went to bed hoping for better progress, but before they were asleep long the ponies began kicking up a fuss. Scrambling out of their tents, the men found that Quan had eaten the straps on one of the rugs put over the ponies to help keep them warm. Grisi and Socks were in the process of fighting over this blanket. Quan had

FROM *The Heart of the Antarctic*

Finnesko boots

also chewed Chinaman's tether in two, and Chinaman was busily savoring the rope. But being less mischievous than Quan, Chinaman hadn't torn up the food bags, which Shackleton believed Quan would have done under similar circumstances. With the ponies secured once more, the men returned to their sleeping bags.

In the morning the ponies started off well on a good hard surface. All of them except Quan seemed improved as a result of the

CANTERBURY MUSEUM

An upturned sledge with a flag marks Shackleton's Depot A on the featureless Barrier.

boiled Maujee ration given them the previous night. Maybe Quan had relished a little too much of the rug and ropes after dinner. The men, on the other hand, struggled with the continual problem of falling on the sastrugi due to the poor light. Shackleton took off his goggles to see better, but he paid the penalty of snow blindness that night. The affliction began by making him see double: "Then the eyes feel full of grit; this makes them water and eventually one cannot see at all."

To their surprise, the men sighted a stray Adélie penguin tobogganing on its belly toward the open sea, one hundred miles away. Where had the penguin come from? they wondered.

The temperature that night (November 10) dropped well below zero and the men woke to a cold −12° F. All of their gear and their finnesko boots, made from reindeer hide, were frozen solid. They were forced to unpack everything and scrape off the sledges, particularly the runners. The ponies also had balls of snow on their feet that had to be removed.

Despite the cold night, the surface on the next day was again very soft with patches of hard sastrugi underneath. Quan suddenly stepped through to one of these rough places and went lame until after lunch when he appeared nearly to have recovered. The men suffered occasional painful snow blindness and burst lips from the wind, but their only worry was locating the first important depot of food laid the previous year. The depot was like a tiny speck in a white desert, sixty miles from the nearest land formation. They had

only the sun and the distant coastal mountains to use in determining their bearings. But when the group camped on November 14, Wild spotted the depot through field glasses and shouted to the others who came running to see. To their great relief, they could see the flag and sledge that marked the cache of four days' pony feed and a gallon of oil for their stove.

They reached the depot the following morning and found everything intact below the flapping flag. In addition to picking up supplies, they left three days' food that they had managed to save, spare gear, and a half-gallon of oil to use on the return journey. Shackleton also decided to cut their excess weight by leaving other provisions, including a tin of sardines and a pot of black currant jam intended as a treat on Christmas Day. Every ounce weighed against their progress. They loaded the maize, which gave the ponies about 450 pounds each to pull on the seldges, except for Quan. The prankster had already been pulling 469 pounds before the depot was reached, so nothing was added to his burden.

Maybe Quan's often goat-like appetite was due to the extra work he was required to do in pulling heavier loads than the other ponies. During the preceding week he had eaten the greater part of a horse rug, six feet of rope, several pieces of leather, and such odds and ends as a nose-bag buckle. But the Boss believed Quan's digestion was marvelous, and the pony thrived on his strange diet. In fact, he "would rather eat a yard of creosoted rope than his maize and Maujee, indeed he often, in sheer wantonness, throws his food all over the snow." Quan's eating habits probably explain why his alias, Blossom, was dropped early in the expedition.

The next day the party departed in "glorious" weather. Despite the −15° F. temperature, the sun was so hot that it dried their reindeer-skin sleeping bags, giving them dry bags to sleep in for a time and a little comfort on their arduous journey. The lips of the explorers were split, which kept them from laughing, but otherwise everyone was in excellent health and hopeful of success. The ponies were working admirably. But a day later, the party once again reached soft snow. Quan plodded stolidly through it, whereas the others had more difficulty, particularly Chinaman, who seemed old and stiff. Chinaman, called the "Vampire" by Adams, was the oldest of the ponies and now his age was beginning to show.

After a day of heavy going, the ponies especially enjoyed their feed that evening. All except Quan, who seemed to show his disgust at not having more Maujee ration and flung his maize out of his nose bag. The men retired, wondering what trouble the ponies would get into during the night.

Right after they fell asleep they found out. One of the ponies began squealing as though the end had come. Shackleton rushed out of his tent to find Socks biting and swallowing lumps of Quan's tail. Had Socks picked up Quan's habits? Or had Quan done something to deserve such unusual treatment? The Boss didn't speculate on this occasion, but one can guess that, not finding a rope handy, sweet "Blossom" had attacked the first thing available. His record was well established. Socks merely retaliated.

Shackleton returned to bed wishing that he had discovered some of the ponies' tricks before the journey so that he could have brought long wire ropes to picket them safely apart.

In the morning there were more serious problems with the ponies. Grisi was found lying down and unable to get up. Having stretched his tether to the end, he couldn't draw back his leg until the men released him. He was shivering with cold, although the temperature was relatively warm, $-5°$ F. All of the ponies had to have the balls of snow that had collected on their hind feet scraped off. Quan, however, didn't appreciate the service. When Shackleton bent down, the prankster chomped on his jacket. Luckily for Quan, the Irishman had his impatience under control.

The temperature rose above zero due to increasing clouds that caused a morning snowstorm. Progress as a result was tediously slow. Hour after hour, the ponies would break through the thin surface crust and flounder up to their hocks in the eight to ten inches of soft snow until they could pull their feet out through the brittle crust. Chinaman, as one would expect, had more trouble than the others. He appeared to be growing older with every mile.

His fetlocks were so severely chafed by the snow crust that Shackleton reluctantly decided he would have to be shot when they established the next depot of supplies in three days.

Shackleton pondered the Antarctic and its strange conditions as the party trekked on:

> It is as though we were truly at the world's end and were bursting in on the birthplace of the clouds and the nesting home of the four winds, and one has a feeling that we mortals are being watched with a jealous eye by the forces of nature. To add to these weird impressions that seem to grow on one in the apparently limitless waste, the sun to-night was surrounded by mock suns and in the zenith was a bow, turning away from the great vertical circle around the sun. These circles and bows were the color of the rainbow.

On November 21, an overcast day, they marched through ice crystals driven into their faces by the wind. Chinaman struggled painfully behind the others. When they camped that evening, the ailing pony had to be destroyed. It was an abhorrent task, even though the men knew the animal had been treated well and made to suffer as little as possible. They built a mound of snow on the lee side of the camp and led Chinaman behind it so the other ponies wouldn't see the killing or smell the blood. The others didn't seem

The Southern Party marching off into the white unknown

FROM *The Heart of the Antarctic*

to pay any attention to the preparations or to the discharge of the revolver held three inches from the victim's forehead. Chinaman died instantly as the sound of the single shot dissipated across the wide open plain of snow. The first pony had died in Antarctica.

Because the party was behind schedule, the rations were being consumed at a faster rate than Shackleton had calculated. If the explorers were to hope to reach the Pole, Chinaman had to be butchered for supplemental food. It was a sad, unpleasant job, although it had been understood from the beginning that they would have to shoot the ponies at some stage on the journey. By this time the ponies had become pets with individual personalities, making the job even more unhappy. But in such a desolate place any food

Shackleton's four ponies, rugged and picketed for the night

FROM *The Heart of the Antarctic*

was too precious to waste. They also thought fresh meat would prevent scurvy, which historically plagued expeditions. For these reasons, the pony's throat was cut immediately to drain the blood, then the carcass was skinned and the men labored to cut up the meat as much as possible into small pieces before it froze. Whenever they had time to spare during the following days, the men continued the butchering until all the meat was prepared for cooking.

Eighty pounds of horse meat, in addition to other supplies, were cached at this camp, Depot B, to see them back to the first depot on the return journey. One of the sledges was stuck up in the snow with a black flag on a bamboo pole lashed to it, marking the depot. Chinaman's harness was used to make stays to anchor the sledge and keep it from being blown down.

When the party continued the next morning, the temperature had risen to 7° F. The ponies were pulling five hundred pounds each through the increasing soft snow. Dr. Marshall wrote that all the ponies were tired and Grisi was "peevish." But they did an admirable job, and Shackleton felt their progress was improving. The day was brilliantly clear, affording the adventurers a view of the unexplored white land to the south. Great snow-clad heights rose beyond the peaks of the coastal mountain range that formed the southern boundary of the ice shelf. For Shackleton this was the land he had toiled so painfully to see on the *Discovery* Expedition with Scott before they had to turn back.

The Southern Party saved its dried provisions at lunch by eating the horse flesh, which the men found tasted like good beef. Wild especially welcomed the meat because he had suffered with an upset stomach for three days and couldn't touch the pemmican, which Scott once described as tasting like a mixture of sawdust and tow, a fiber used in making cloth. Adams also was suffering; he with a wisdom tooth that had given him so much pain that he hadn't been able to sleep at night for some time. Although they weren't equipped for any dental work, Dr. Marshall tried to pull the tooth, which broke off, causing Adams even greater pain until the next day when the doctor succeeded in removing it. Adams subsequently joined the others in enjoying fried horse steaks at the evening meal.

72

5 A Valiant Effort

COVERING seventeen miles of new territory each day, the ponies performed well as the Southern Party marched on across the Barrier, which Shackleton described as "still as level as a billiard table." The men had frozen raw horse flesh to eat while underway, and it helped to cool their throats in the hot sun. For the evening meal they cooked the meat into a hoosh that they ate with pemmican biscuits. Wild's condition was improving, and Adams reported a new wisdom tooth growing in place of the one that had been extracted so painfully.

The explorers marveled at the lofty coastal mountain peaks rising over ten thousand feet to their right and continuing to the southeast. Wondering what they might discover, the men's imaginations "would take wings until a stumble in the snow, the sharp pangs of hunger, or the dull ache of physical weariness" brought back their attention. Their feeling of insignificance increased as mountain after mountain came into view. "We were but tiny black specks crawling slowly and painfully across the white plain, and bending our puny strength to the task of wrestling from nature secrets preserved inviolate through all the ages," Shackleton wrote.

The Boss began to worry as another great range appeared to the southeast, threatening to cut across their path. Would there be an entry point among the series of inlets and capes that made up the

coastline? There had to be, because the party wasn't equipped to do any mountain climbing.

Although the new land gave Shackleton reason to be concerned, the sight of it coming closer each day helped to relieve the boredom that the men felt during the long hours of trudging across the ice shelf. But the ponies didn't understand the reason or the reward for their drudgery. They appeared to Shackleton to feel the monotony, and at times he noticed them looking at the distant land.

On November 26, they passed the point that Scott had previously established as the furthest south any man had reached, Latitude 82° 16½′S., on December 30, 1902. When they broke camp that morning, all signs were encouraging. The weather had warmed up to 19° F., enabling the men to dry their sleeping bags. But then Quan had a sharp attack of colic as they were preparing to start. Fortunately, the pony was well enough to pull about an hour later. Shackleton viewed the cause of the illness as the beast's "morbid craving for bits of rope and other odds and ends in preference to his proper food." That night, they celebrated breaking Scott's record with two tablespoons each of curaçao liqueur and a smoke before turning in.

The warmer temperatures, at first welcome, soon became a major problem. The surface of the ice shelf was so soft that it nearly

Mountains of the "new land" can be seen faintly in the background as the Southern Party camps after passing the furthest point south anyone had ever been.

began to melt, and the poor ponies sank ever deeper into the snow layer. In addition, snow blindness afflicted both men and ponies as the glaring sun reflected unchecked off the crystalline surface. Grisi, the most spirited, healthy pony, was particularly affected by the snow blindness, and it put him off his food. He had become exhausted and his vision severely impaired. There was no hope now for Grisi. When the party camped on November 28, he was shot and butchered.

The men then established Depot C, containing one week's provisions, including horse meat, to carry them back to the depot where Chinaman had been killed. They had enough food left for 63 days, and 1425 miles to go to the Pole and back to base. Wild by this time was nearly convinced that if the party got to the Pole, they wouldn't make it back in time to be picked up by the *Nimrod* when it returned for them. The ponies obviously wouldn't last much beyond Depot C, even though they had covered only about 370 miles in less than a month.

The next morning, the men loaded 630 pounds on each of two sledges. The party needed a hard surface to make good headway, but the snow layer became increasingly soft during the march, particularly in the hollows of great undulations through which they were passing. At one time in the afternoon the ponies sank up to

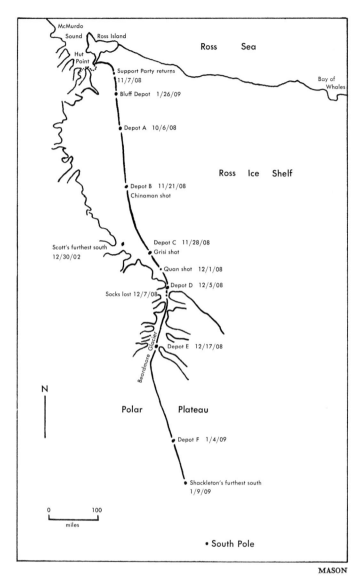

McMurdo
Sound
Ross Island
Hut
Point
Support Party returns
11/7/08
Bluff Depot 1/26/09

Depot A 10/6/08

Depot B 11/21/08
Chinaman shot

Scott's furthest south
12/30/02
Depot C 11/28/08
Grisi shot

Quan shot 12/1/08
Depot D 12/5/08
Socks lost 12/7/08

Depot E 12/17/08

Beardmore Glacier

N

Polar   Plateau

Depot F 1/4/09

Shackleton's furthest south
1/9/09

0   100
miles

South Pole

Ross   Sea

Bay of
Whales

Ross   Ice   Shelf

MASON

Route of the Southern Party toward the South Pole

their bellies, and the men had to pull with all their strength to move
the sledges. The ponies were played out by six o'clock, even the
energetic Quan. He nearly collapsed from the struggle of lifting his

76

legs through the soft snow. Both ponies were also snow blinded and the men improvised eyeshades in an effort to help them.

Quan appeared shaky and on his last legs when the party started on the morning of November 30. The men took turns, one on each side, helping him pull the sledge. Socks and his handlers, meanwhile, would get ahead and have the opportunity for a short rest while Quan and his two helpers caught up. That evening at camp the ponies were given extra food, but they didn't eat it all. Quan enjoyed his Maujee ration but neglected the maize.

Quan was so weak the next day that three of the men, stripped to their shirts, virtually pulled his sledge as they tried to assist him. After lunch, Wild led Quan and Socks with one sledge, while the other men teamed up to haul the other. But old Quan, the prankster, was finished. To end his suffering he was shot and butchered when the party camped for the day, December 1. Shackleton was particularly sad at losing Quan because he had been his special horse since March. Despite his annoying tricks, Quan was the favorite pony and had seemed unusually intelligent.

The temperature was a "hot" 16° F. and the sun beat down on them as the explorers continued the next day, the men pulling one sledge followed by Socks hauling the other. Wearing shirts and pajama trousers, the men perspired heavily while their feet were cold in the snow. They were also forced to wear their goggles all the time to protect their eyes from the intense glare. Although the scene around them was pure grandeur, with more new mountain peaks and the moon visible in the sky, they began to feel increasingly hungry and daydreamed about what they would do if let loose in a good restaurant.

They stopped at lunch and cooked some of Quan's meat, which turned out to be very tough, due perhaps to the condition of the pony when he was shot. Surprisingly Socks, whose lameness had delayed the start of the journey, had outlasted the other ponies. Socks appeared quite lonely and whinnied all night for his lost companion. How much sleep the men got that night Shackleton didn't record.

On December 3, the four men left Socks with a full day's supply of food and climbed a red hill about three thousand feet high, now called Mount Hope, to survey the surrounding area. As they suspected, the ice shelf on which they had been traveling was bounded by a great chain of coastal mountains. But then they made the most important discovery of the expedition. They saw a great glacier flowing through a nearby gap in the mountains that appeared to be a highway leading to the South Pole. Such an expansive river of ice had never been seen before. Although another glacier in Antarctica has since been found to be larger, the mighty Beardmore, one hundred miles in length and in places forty miles wide, is staggering to behold. (As the name indicates, Shackleton used the occasion to honor his principal financial supporter.) The only drawback to using this route to the Pole might be Socks's inability to pull a sledge up it. The men wanted to avoid hauling the sledge themselves because it meant relay work that would take precious time and consume their food. Relaying was necessary as a safety precaution on the heavily crevassed glacier.

After returning from Mount Hope, the party started a difficult trek from the ice shelf up a steep snow slope to get onto the actual glacier. Three of the men pulled one sledge while Wild, leading Socks, followed in their wake, a protective measure to prevent losing all their supplies in a crevasse. Their caution soon proved to be warranted. Dr. Marshall suddenly fell up to his arms in a chasm and was saved only because he was able to hold himself up by his outstretched arms until the others came to the rescue.

The men were pleased with their accomplishment when they camped for the day and excited by the prospect of becoming the first to reach the very bottom of the world. Socks, however, wasn't eating well and still appeared lonely. They gave him a drink of thaw water, but he preferred to eat the snow at his feet. At this camp the Southern Party established Depot D on December 5.

Shackleton, Adams, and Dr. Marshall began making their way down an icy slope to the glacier itself the next morning. Suddenly, their sledge started skidding rapidly, even though the men put on

FROM *The Heart of the Antarctic*

*Approaching the newly discovered mountains, which Shackleton named
the Queen Alexandra Range for the Queen of England, the Southern
Party discovered a great glacier flowing through a gap in the mountains
(center right) like a highway leading to the polar plateau of the interior.*

the rope brakes and hung onto it as best they could. Since the
danger had been exposed, Wild took Socks and carefully circum-
vented the slope by a snow route.

At the bottom of this slope, the men gawked at 2000-foot pillars
of granite on either side of them. Fantastically shaped ice ridges
were massed in front of them, blocking their path. They soon found
a gentle snow slope, along which they proceeded, but this gave way
to blue ice full of small crevasses. Fearing Socks might step in one
and break a leg, they unharnessed him and Wild guided him carefully over the impasse. The others hauled first one, then the other,
sledge across to safety.

For the next two days they traveled up and down slopes, with
Shackleton, Adams, and Marshall pulling one sledge while Wild led

79

Socks with the other. The weakening pony sank up to his belly in very deep snow, and the men continuously plunged in and out of it. Despite the poor light due to a partially overcast sky, they could see threatening crevasses on either side of their trail. Several times Socks stepped through the bridges of concealed crevices that the men, being lighter, had walked over without breaking through them. Leading the pony, Wild felt "rather uneasy." He knew that at any moment he might plummet into an abyss, especially because Socks constantly required holding back.

At lunchtime on December 7, the party was forced by poor light to camp, despite a crevasse five yards on either side of them. The light improved after lunch and they continued on, congratulating themselves on this piece of good luck. Following about ten yards behind the others, Wild suddenly stepped into space. He felt a rush of something past him and a "vicious snatch" at his right hand. The next moment he found himself hanging only by his left arm from the edge of a "horrible chasm." Shouting for help, he managed to pull himself out as the other men ran to him. They quickly got the sledge with its broken bow to safety, but Socks was gone.

Although the men lay down on their stomachs and peered over into the gulf, they couldn't see or hear anything in the "black bottomless pit." The weight of Socks apparently had snapped the sledge crossbar, saving Wild and the sledge from tumbling into the crevasse along with the pony. It was a miraculous escape for the young explorer but a disaster for the expedition. Gone was the horse meat that they had counted on to sustain them during the remainder of the trek. Although they were saddened by the loss of Socks, the pony couldn't have been taken much further because of poor traction on the glacier ice. In fact, Shackleton's intention had been to have the animal shot that very evening.

Hitching themselves to the traces, the men started off, pulling one thousand pounds between them on the two sledges, including the ponies' maize that they now would have to eat themselves. For ten days the four Britons dragged the sledges up more than one hundred miles of the heavily crevassed, rough terrain of the Beardmore. They encountered every variety of alpine surface from soft snow to cracked and hard blue ice. Crevasses were the only constant feature.

The intrepid men roped themselves together for safety as they continued to negotiate steep slopes and precipitous ice ridges. At times they had to cut steps with ice axes and haul the sledges up after them. Often the going was so difficult that they had to work in relays, advancing half a mile with one sledge, then returning for the other. Falling into a crevasse became so commonplace that when one tumbled into an abyss the others would inquire casually, "Have you found it?" They were saved on many occasions from being lost in a crevasse by their sledges, which often bridged the openings of the fearful cracks. Luckily, the weather was on their side. All would have been lost if a storm had struck while they were on the glacier. Flying over the Beardmore today, one is amazed that anyone could have made his way up such a treacherous river of ice. Surely the ponies could never have made it.

In addition to the backbreaking effort, the explorers were marching hungry, with only five weeks of food left and 1190 miles to cover to the Pole and back to base. To make their food last longer, they ground the pony maize into flour from which they made little patties. Much was lost in the grinding, but they couldn't afford to use their precious oil to boil the maize to soften and cook it. So they ate it raw, hoping it would swell inside their stomachs and reduce their steadily increasing hunger.

By December 17, they were six thousand feet up the glacier but disappointed they hadn't reached the polar plateau. "One more crevassed slope and we will be on the plateau, please God," Shackleton wrote. Here they established Depot E, called Upper Glacier Depot, two-thirds of the way up the glacier and left their extra clothes and four days of the shortened rations. They didn't expect to climb much higher, but their ordeal was far from over.

Temperatures began to drop with the ascent and the wind was persistent, causing frostbitten ears, faces, and fingers. They thought of little else but food.

Each day when they camped after ten strenuous hours of hauling, the men took unusual care to make sure everyone was satisfied that the little pans of hoosh and the biscuits were divided equally. Not a crumb was wasted. If someone dropped a fragment of biscuit, the others were quick to point it out, and the owner would wet his finger and pick up the morsel as though it were a treasure. When the pony meat was used in the hoosh, the cook had to take extra care in making the divisions because the little dices of meat sank to the bottom of the pot. Even though the meat was usually tough and stringy, it was relished by the four hungry men.

The Southern Party finally emerged out of the crevassed area of the glacier on Christmas Eve, giving them the hope of a better surface to speed their progress. When they camped under great rock cliffs on Christmas Day, they had reached an altitude of 9500 feet. In a temperature of $-18°$ F. they celebrated with what they considered a splendid dinner. They enjoyed a hoosh of pony maize boiled with pemmican and some bullion with biscuits. For dessert they boiled a little plum pudding in cocoa water, to which they added some medicinal brandy. With a cup of steaming cocoa they smoked cigars and had a spoonful each of crème de menthe. It was their first full meal in forty days. But in a couple of hours they felt as hungry as ever.

After the meal, the group made the difficult decision to further reduce their daily rations of food and to dump everything they didn't absolutely need, which amounted to about forty pounds. They had five hundred miles to cover to the Pole and back to this camp. It was "now or never," as Dr. Marshall put it.

Unknown to Shackleton and his campanions, they had already passed the head of the Beardmore and had been on the polar plateau that forms the glacier for several days. They were misled by the continuing uphill battle with pressure ridges and crevasses impeding their progress. Their clothes were weathered thin and

Aerial view of one section of treacherous terrain on the Beardmore Glacier surface

U.S. NAVY

patched from being torn on the ice, and their boots were nearly worn out. Their heels were frostbitten, particularly Shackleton's, whose burst and caked his socks with blood until Marshall devised some bandages. Their fingers quickly froze when they tried to hoist a sail on their sledge to take advantage of the wind. If this wasn't enough, their body temperatures were dropping and the high altitude gave them headaches, forcing them to lie down for a few minutes during their hourly breaks. They were also plagued with indigestion, undoubtedly due to the hard pony maize. "Otherwise we are fit and well!" Shackleton insisted.

His determined optimism, however, was slowly subdued by "the strongest forces of Nature." Although the surface began to level off, there were low temperatures and strong winds that stymied them; on the last day of the year a blizzard kept them tent-bound. On January 1, 1909, they struggled eleven miles through soft snow to gain 87°S., the furthest point north or south man had reached. They were now 10,755 feet above sea level and two hundred statute miles from the Pole.

On the next day, the Boss realized defeat was inevitable. They weren't traveling fast enough on their allotted food to make the Pole and return to Depot E on the upper part of the Beardmore. "I cannot think of failure yet I must look at the matter sensibly and the lives of those who are with me." Sinking up to eight inches in the snow layer, the men labored across the plateau until January 4. Then they decided to gamble and leave their sledge, marked only by a bamboo pole with a piece of bag sewn on it. They continued on foot, trusting their footprints would lead them back to this cache, Depot F, on the vast featureless plain. They gained the advantage of not having to drag the sledge behind them, which Shackleton called a nightmare, but they unfortunately didn't get far before a three-day blizzard stymied them on January 6.

Although the storm swept the surface, leaving it hard and easier to travel on, the men were so exhausted and weak from hunger that the benefit meant little to their progress. "We have shot our bolt," Shackleton realized on the morning of January 9 when the storm

FROM *The Heart of the Antarctic*

Their beards frosted with ice, three of the Southern Party pose beside the Union Jack, claiming the polar plateau for England.

abated. Yet, determined to reach as close as possible to the Pole, they took two Union Jack flags and, leaving their camp, made a final push south. At a point 112 miles from the Pole the defeated explorers stopped and looked south with powerful binoculars. But they could see nothing except "the dead white snow plain." They guessed correctly that the South Pole lay there, just beyond them. They had come so far and endured so much that it must have been a crushing defeat. If only Socks had not been lost in the crevasse, they might have had food enough to make it.

The four stayed only a few minutes after claiming possession of the polar plateau for England. Eating a scanty meal as they went, they hurried back toward the camp. Fortunately their tracks were easy to follow and they arrived at their tent safely. After packing up, they marched back to Depot F, where they picked up their sledge. By erecting a sail on the sledge, they traveled more easily back across the plateau toward the Beardmore, although the sledge would often overrun them.

A seven-week race against starvation now began. They were down to a ration of two spoonfuls of cheese, one and a half biscuits, and a cup of tea at each meal. Shackleton speculated that in the cities of civilization anyone as hungry as they were wouldn't be deterred by any barrier of law and order from obtaining food.

The battered men arrived sore and aching at Upper Glacier Depot on January 20. Their shaky sledge had only half a runner left on one side. And they had barely enough food to last them until the next depot, forty miles across crevasses down the Beardmore. Five days later, they came to the end of their provisions, a pannikin of pony maize. They had nothing but cocoa and tea during January 26 and 27 when they traversed the worst surfaces and most dangerous crevasses on the expedition. They also encountered snow from a recent storm that averaged ten to eighteen inches and sometimes was as much as thirty inches deep. Only their harnesses by which they pulled the sledge saved them after repeated falls into the hidden pits.

When the exhausted men camped on January 27, Dr. Marshall pushed on a half-mile to Depot D, established near the bottom of the glacier. He brought back pony meat, cheese, hoosh, biscuits, and tobacco. "Never did men enjoy a meal more," he observed. In a few days, however, they were to suffer for this meal.

The four started in the morning after allowing time for photographs and to collect some additional rock specimens. By lunchtime they reached the Gap, the pass by which they had got on the Beardmore. Shackleton fell into the last crevasse on the glacier, which seemed to him to be a warning not to return.

At Depot D, the party collected all the food supply, including some pony meat, which was enough for six days. Since there were only about fifty miles to go to the next depot, the men considered themselves safe. The temperature was up to 26° F. They only had to worry about snowstorms, which the Boss knew were prevalent at that time of the year. Then, as if to remind them the journey wasn't over yet, Wild reported sick with dysentery, and the ice shelf greeted them in the late afternoon with a two-day blizzard. They

FROM *The Heart of the Antarctic*

Lower Glacier Depot D

waited anxiously in their tents, patching their clothes and wondering if they would be able to find the next depot.

Although Wild wasn't well, they were forced to push on after the storm. The following day he was too sick to pull and had to walk beside the sledge. Dr. Marshall gave him some medicine, but it made him drowsy and he kept falling asleep on the march. Because their food allowance was critical, Wild couldn't have any more of the biscuit, even though it was the only thing he could eat and keep down. Privately, Shackleton took his one breakfast biscuit and forced Wild to accept it. That night Wild wrote in his diary that he would never forget how much generosity and sympathy were shown by this. ". . . BY GOD I shall never forget it. Thousands of pounds would not have bought that one biscuit."

When the party camped at Depot C, where Grisi had been shot, Shackleton was also suffering with dysentery and was dead tired from marching while weakened by the illness. At the depot they picked up a sledge to replace their battered one and 150 pounds of

87

provisions, including more horse meat. They also scraped the meat off Grisi's bones, which had been lying in the sun for more than a month. This meat they decided not to risk eating until there was absolutely nothing else.

The following day when they started with their new sledge the heavy snow conditions on the ice shelf had improved. But now all of them were suffering with dysentery. Shackleton's condition became so bad that he couldn't pull the sledge and had to walk alongside it. Despite their state, the men continued to transport the geological specimens taken from the mountain walls of the Beardmore. On February 4, they were unable to march at all and lay in camp with acute diarrhea.

The dysentery stopped two days later, but the men continued eating the pony meat because of their hunger. They had to have food to keep going. The next day, Adams and Marshall had dysentery again, although Shackleton and Wild were unaffected. This led Shackleton to believe the dysentery was caused by eating meat from Grisi, who had been shot in an exhausted condition, causing toxins to spread through his body. Those who didn't develop the illness were the ones fortunate enough not to receive a tainted portion of meat when the hoosh was dished out.

The party continued sixty-nine miles to Chinaman Depot, which they reached on February 13. They cooked the pony's liver and looked around the old campsite for scraps of meat. Digging in the snow, they found a solid core of frozen blood. They boiled it and found it tasted like beef tea.

After another two days of trudging across the ice shelf, the men were again appallingly hungry. They were down to half a pannikin of partially cooked horse meat and four biscuits a day. They were so weak they could hardly lift the depleted provision bag, make camp, or even pick up their feet. Their frostbitten fingers were blistered and painful; their vesicated lips had burst.

Food taunted them in their dreams for the next four days. At mealtimes, the men would look angrily at anyone who made his portion last longer than the others. By February 19, they had no food except the scraps from Grisi's bones, which they still feared to eat. "Our food lies ahead and death stalks us from behind," Shackleton lamented.

Fortunately, the party reached Depot A the following evening, and they had what they considered a feast: hoosh, biscuits and jam, and a smoke afterward. The Boss, however, knew they still didn't have enough food to make it back unless another cache, Bluff Depot, had been laid by the support party waiting on Ross Island. Whether the depot had been established and whether they could find it were nagging questions.

The famished men again were short of food the next day and were forced to stew the Grisi scraps. But on the following day they came across tracks of dogs and men, assuring them the support party had made Bluff Depot. All the food they could possibly eat waited for them in the white distance. A day later, the depot appeared in a mirage, taunting them. They knew it was close because Mount Erebus and other landmarks had come into view. But they were prevented from hurrying by a renewed case of dysentery that Wild had come down with during the night. They were forced to plod their way slowly toward their salvation, as if the troublesome ponies were still with them.

When they reached Bluff Depot, they weren't disappointed. There they found boiled mutton, eggs, and cakes! All they had to do was restrain themselves from overeating, which wasn't easy. As they pushed on across the ice shelf, they believed their troubles were over at last. Wild's dysentery was improving. Then, two days later, on February 25, Dr. Marshall came down with it and suffered a terrible paralysis of the stomach. To make matters worse, a blizzard trapped them in their tents for two very miserable days.

They tried to continue after the storm, but Marshall's condition was worse. So Shackleton left him with Adams and pushed on with Wild. As they approached Hut Point their food was gone, and both Shackleton and Wild were suffering with frostbitten feet. It was a crucial moment. They were late returning and they knew the relief ship must be preparing to depart without them. Deciding to aban-

FROM *The Heart of the Antarctic*

Safe on board the Nimrod (left to right), *Frank Wild, Ernest Shackleton, Eric Marshall, and Jameson Adams*

don the sledge, they made a dash for the old Scott quarters. The gamble paid off. They reached Hut Point in the nick of time and were picked up by the *Nimrod*. Then, with very little rest, Shackleton led a rescue party to bring home Marshall and Adams. The reunion on board the ship on March 3 was particularly joyous because a party headed by David had completed a grueling trek of twelve hundred miles to claim the South Magnetic Pole and return.

Shackleton arrived home as a hero. The crowds were uncontrollable when his train pulled into London on June 14, 1909. After making a speech, he was forced to stand up and show himself in the carriage as the driver tried to make way through the mass. According to legend, the people unharnessed the horses and, forming themselves into teams, pulled the carriage themselves. What a greater triumph it would have been if only the ponies could have survived to draw the great explorer's carriage that day.

PART TWO

Scott's Ponies

Training sledge found at Cape Evans

BRITISH ANTARCTIC (*TERRA NOVA*) EXPEDITION, 1910–1912

Primary Staff

Robert Falcon Scott	Captain, R.N.; leader
George P. Abbott	Petty Officer, R.N.
W. W. Archer	Chief Steward
Edward L. Atkinson	Surgeon, R.N.; parasitologist
Henry R. Bowers	Lieutenant, Royal Indian Marines; stores manager
Frank V. Browning	Petty Officer, R.N.
Wilfred Bruce	Lieutenant, R.N.
Victor L. A. Campbell	Lieutenant, R.N.
Apsley Cherry-Garrard	Assistant zoologist
Thomas Clissold	Cook
Thomas Crean	Petty Officer, N.R.
Bernard C. Day	Motor engineer
Frank Debenham	Geologist
Harry Dickason	Able Seaman, R.N.
Edgar Evans	Petty Officer, R.N.
Edward R. G. R. Evans	Lieutenant, R.N.
Robert Forde	Petty Officer, R.N.
Demetri Gerof	Russian dog driver
Tryggve Gran	Sub-Lieutenant, Norwegian Naval Reserve; ski expert
F. J. Hopper	Steward
Patrick Keohane	Petty Officer, R.N.
William Lashly	Chief Stoker, R.N.
G. Murray Levick	Surgeon, R.N.
Cecil H. Meares	In charge of dogs
Edward W. Nelson	Biologist
Lawrence E. G. Oates	Captain, Inniskilling Dragoons; in charge of ponies
Anton Omelchenko	Russian groom
Herbert G. Ponting	Photographer
Raymond E. Priestley	Geologist
George C. Simpson	Meteorologist
T. Griffith Taylor	Geologist
Thomas S. Williamson	Petty Officer, R.N.
Edward A. Wilson	Zoologist; chief of scientific staff
Charles S. Wright	Physicist

New Zealand Trainer: J. Thomas

Ponies:

Blossom	Christopher	Jehu	Nobby	Uncle Bill
Blucher	Davy	Jimmy Pigg	Punch	Victor
Bones	Guts	Jones	Snatcher	Weary Willy
Chinaman	Hackenschmidt	Michael	Snippets	

Mules: Abdullah, Begam, Gulab, Khan Sahib, Lal Khan, Pyaree, Rani

6 One More Time

AFTER Ernest Shackleton's return from the Antarctic, English newspapers almost immediately began to speculate that he wouldn't rest long before attempting another journey to the South Pole. The Irishman had demonstrated that the Pole could be reached, and the race was on to win the honor of getting there first. Belgium, Germany, Japan, France, and the United States were mounting expeditions, as well as England. The prize had become even greater because the North Pole had been attained a few months before Shackleton's arrival home, although a bitter controversy raged over which of two explorers had been the first to see the top of the world.

The leading contender for the South Pole, Robert Scott, had been organizing his second Antarctic venture for two years, during which time he was involved in testing tracked motor vehicles. The same type of tractor-like machine, which became the forerunner of the tank, had been used successfully in Norway. Spurred by the widening international eyes on the Pole, Scott had to shift his plans into high gear. On September 13, 1909, the Royal Navy captain announced his intentions of establishing a base at McMurdo Sound or on King Edward VII Land. To appease scientists and politicians, the scientific aspects of his expedition were emphasized so that it would not appear to be an all-out scramble for the Pole, which in fact Scott wanted to avoid.

For transportation during his attempt on the Pole, Scott decided on a combination of the experimental tracked vehicles, Manchurian ponies, dogs, and man-hauling. He adopted Shackleton's innovation of using ponies to cross the Ross Ice Shelf, despite the Irishman's trouble with them. Shackleton had stated on his return to New Zealand that gaining the Pole was just a matter of more ponies and more provisions. The performance of the ponies was never questioned. In fact, the *Lyttelton Times*, which had interviewed the Boss, claimed he had shown that Manchurian ponies could do "brilliant work on the surface of the great Ice Barrier." But their unsuitability for glacier work through the mountains to the Pole was also regarded as proved. For the final leg of the journey Scott considered, then rejected, the idea of using dogs. Although dogs were taken in a supporting role, Scott believed the best and most noble way was for the men to haul the sledges themselves. Dogs he deemed unreliable due to his earlier experience with them, and he was too sensitive to drive them to death or to use the weakening dogs to feed the stronger ones during the trek. On the other hand, he had no qualms about killing the dogs or the ponies if the men needed them as food to stay alive or to prevent scurvy.

Scott's exasperating time with dogs, however, had been preceded by an earlier encounter with a pony. When he was about eight years old, he rode to school on his own pony Beppo, known for bucking off all riders except Scott, who always managed to stay on somehow. One day, Scott dismounted to gaze over a gate at a view that impressed him. Beppo meanwhile trotted off. Scott walked seven miles home, stopping at police stations to give details of his loss and a description of the wayward pony.

The ponies that Scott purchased for his expedition proved to be of similar character but far more obstreperous. He sent Lieutenant Wilfred Bruce, his brother-in-law and one of the expedition's ship officers, to northern China, where Bruce bought nineteen ponies at

Captain Robert Falcon Scott
SCOTT POLAR RESEARCH INSTITUTE

the city of Harbin. The lieutenant was assisted by a jockey, Anton Omelchenko, whom he met at the Russian port of Vladivostok and hired to help care for the ponies. Because of Shackleton's report that light-colored ponies had been the more hardy, Bruce selected only those that were white or dappled gray. Some members of the expedition later criticized him for trusting too much of the decision-making (other than that of color) to a local dealer and a veterinarian.

Standing fourteen to fifteen hands high, the ponies were purchased with money donated by various schools, clubs, and individuals, for whom they were named. Each in time was also given a nickname by the men of the expedition. Scott called the ponies Siberian, but according to Apsely Cherry-Garrard, the venture's assistant zoologist, only two were Siberian and the others came from Manchuria, as Shackleton's had. Cherry-Garrard also noted

95

that most were too big to be classified as ponies, although Scott always referred to them so.

The ponies were assembled at Vladivostok along with thirty-one Siberian and two Eskimo sledge dogs. The expedition's dog handler, Cecil Meares, had driven the canines across Siberia with the help of a young Russian dog driver, Demetri Gerof. Rain was pouring down and the quay was inches deep in mud when all the animals were ready to board a Japanese steamer on July 26, 1910, nearly two months after the expedition's ship, the *Terra Nova*, had sailed from London. Two of the ponies broke away twice, but Anton recaptured them and eventually the truants were coaxed into the horse box for loading. Anton sat on the back of one of these ponies while Bruce tried to tie a rope around its head. Without warning the pony reared and came down with a foreleg on each of Bruce's shoulders. The ponies fortunately weren't shod, and Bruce was hurt much less than he feared.

The handlers finally realized that treating the wild ponies gently and carefully was the wrong approach and began to use brute force. Soaked to the skin and covered with mud from head to foot, the men finished hoisting the ponies aboard the steamer after eight hours of hard work.

All of the ponies had been given the Mallein test for glanders, a highly contagious and very destructive disease of horses character- ized by ulcers. One pony, the twentieth selected, was suspect and had to be left behind. The expedition couldn't chance having the disease transmitted to the other animals or to the men.

At Kobe, Japan, the animals were transferred from the Japanese steamer to a German passenger ship, because no British shipping company would take them. And for good reason. Although the handlers did their best to keep everything clean, the dogs reeked, and they frequently howled in unison during the night. The men, to say the least, weren't very popular among the passengers on the German vessel.

After several ports of call, the animals arrived in Australia, where crowds first began coming to see what Bruce described as "only very ordinary ponies and rather exceptionally fierce dogs." Demetri, however, gave a different view later in a story he told some of the men in the Antarctic. While visiting the ship in Sydney, a funny old man and his wife had objected to Demetri's whipping the dogs, which were "more than half wolf." This couple then proceeded to the ponies. Giving Anton a cigarette, the man pointed to a pony that was lighter and more handsome than the others and asked its age. Since the Russian jockey didn't know, they went to try to check its teeth. The pony reared and, rushing forward, bit the old man, who fell backward over a case, thus establishing the vicious character of the pony called Hackenschmidt.

The ponies inevitably were wobbly when they arrived at Port Lyttelton on September 15 for transfer to quarantine on Quail Island. They had stood without being allowed to lie down for fifty-two days because, as in the case of Shackleton's ponies, the experts advised it. But once ashore in New Zealand, the ponies quickly regained their strength. They fought and kicked each other every chance they got until the handlers separated them.

Scott and the expedition arrived aboard the *Terra Nova* about six weeks later (October 28). In Melbourne, Australia, where Scott

Ponies being transferred at Port Lyttelton

had rejoined the ship after traveling separately from England, he received devastating news. The famous Norwegian explorer Roald Amundsen had cabled Scott to announce his intention of trying for the South Pole too. This news was a bombshell. Nearly everyone, including most of Amundsen's staff, believed he was proceeding on a planned exploration of the Arctic. But word having come during his preparations that Peary's band had gained the North Pole, Amundsen secretly changed his plans, even though his expedition was already underway. Scott's carefully determined expedition, emphasizing an extensive scientific program, was now threatened. Although the English leader was deeply worried because he knew his exploration would seem insignificant if Amundsen reached the Pole first, he decided to continue as he originally planned. Amundsen in his cable to Scott did not reveal where he proposed to establish his base. Scott believed the Norwegian's route via Argentina meant he would launch his attempt from the opposite side of Antarctica.

At Lyttelton, Scott and his men began four hectic weeks of preparations for the voyage south. The New Zealanders (most of whom were British descendants) rallied to the cause and donated two to three times as many supplies as Scott listed that they needed, including pony fodder. Captain Lawrence Oates of the Inniskilling Dragoons took charge of the ponies, with the help of the groom, Anton, and Mr. J. Thomas, a New Zealand horse trainer. Oates, thirty years old, was known as Titus or as "the Soldier." Being an officer of a cavalry regiment, he knew horses well and had gained experience with them in South Africa during the Boer War and in India. In fact, it has been said that he thought more of horses and dogs than of their masters.

Oates was one of the few on the Scott expedition who didn't view Amundsen's actions as underhanded. It wasn't underhanded to keep his mouth shut, he wrote to his mother. Oates was optimistic about the "Norskies'" chances, adding that "if Scott does anything silly such as underfeeding his ponies he will be beaten sure as death." Oates consequently pestered Scott until the leader agreed to

*Roald Engelbregt
Gravning Amundsen*

take on more pony fodder at the expense of some of the coal needed to fuel the *Terra Nova*. Scott had planned to take thirty tons of compressed wheat, purchased in Melbourne, and the Soldier persuaded him to add five tons each of hay, oil cake, and bran. Later, Oates managed to smuggle an additional two tons of fodder on board, most likely with the help of Lieutenant Henry Bowers, the short, indefatigable organizer of the stores who became particularly fond of the ponies. In fact, the 27-year-old Royal Indian Marine was accused during Scott's journey to the Pole of over-provisioning the animals.

When Oates first saw the ponies, he called them first class, although he didn't examine them carefully. He later discovered that some were too old and in poor shape; they should not have been bought. In the opinion of Dr. Edward Wilson, the expedition's zoologist and chief of the scientific staff, the pony selection was

99

ALEXANDER TURNBULL LIBRARY

Scott (left) *and Oates* (third from left) *view a pony's progress.*

limited by the belief that the white-colored ones were more hardy. The buyers had followed Scott's instructions, but they obviously hadn't known what they were doing. If Oates had picked the ponies, they undoubtedly would have been better ones and the fate of the expedition might have been different. As it was, they had few decent ponies, as Wilson and Cherry-Garrard agreed. Not only were some "old as the hills" but also the ponies had suffered a life of "ill-treatment, hard work, and poor food." Further, they were troubled by laminitis, an inflammation of the hoof, according to Wilson. This ailment should have caused greater concern than it apparently did, for lameness often results. Moreover, a pony that has been stricken with laminitis is more susceptible to getting it again.

It is difficult to believe that the handlers didn't notice the ponies' condition while they were being broken in at Lyttelton. Maybe they thought the ponies would perk up with rest and proper care, or maybe they were misled by the animals' wildness. Under the cir-

100

cumstances, however, it seems that the handlers may have been guilty of wishful thinking. With the eyes of the other explorers on the Pole, there was no time to find replacements. Also, too much work and money had gone into mounting the expedition to abandon it at the last minute because one aspect of the transport was in doubt.

As preparations continued for the ship's departure, the ponies were more or less tamed. Then the handlers worked with them every morning at the task of pulling sledges. A few special visitors were invited to observe, including the governor of New Zealand and Kathleen Scott who, like a few of the wives, had accompanied her husband to New Zealand.

The nineteen ponies were put aboard a lighter at Quail Island on November 25 and towed by a launch to the Lyttelton wharf where they waited overnight. They were loaded aboard the *Terra Nova* the next morning and wedged into wooden stalls. Fifteen were put under the forecastle. Since that was the maximum number the space could hold, the remaining four were housed on the port side of the forehatch. Four to five tons of fodder were packed tightly in the narrow irregular space at the front of the ship, which provided a

Oates (left) *and Kathleen Scott join the Captain* (center) *as he inspects the ponies on Quail Island.*

snug nest for three pet rabbits. Also aboard were thirty-three huskies, the ship's cat, a Persian kitten, a guinea pig, a pigeon, and some
squirrels. The menagerie prompted Lieutenant Edward Evans, the
second-in-command, to describe the ship as a floating farmyard.

When the *Terra Nova* left Lyttelton on November 26, a local
reporter described the ponies as maintaining "a severely exparte
attitude and while their noses were being stroked, ate chaff unceas-
ingly." The ship sailed down the coast to Port Chalmers, from
where the expedition finally departed on November 29.

As Shackleton's had, Scott's expedition got its first taste of the
rough seas south of New Zealand after two days. The *Terra Nova*,
an ancient whaler, pitched and rolled, its masts careening from side
to side. Through the worst of it, Anton bravely stood watch under
the forecastle with eight ponies on one side and seven on the other.
Scott peeked through a hole in the bulkhead on occasion to see "a
row of heads with sad, patient eyes come swinging up together from
the starboard side" while those on the port side swung back. Then
up would come the port heads while those on the starboard side
receded.

Although he feared the strain of standing there for weeks would
affect the ponies' condition, Scott wrote in his diary that their trial
couldn't be judged by human standards. He believed the ponies
were the type of horses that never lie down, because they possessed
a ligament in each leg which took "their weight without strain."
Obviously the experts had given Scott incorrect advice. Ponies are
able to sleep standing up, but they much prefer to lie down. This
unintentional mistreatment, compounding the ponies' history of
abuse, surely contributed to their bad temperament and poor condition.

There was little doubt about Anton's condition, however. Suffering badly from seasickness, the groom rubbed his stomach and said
to Oates, "No good." Between intervals of vomiting he tried smoking a cigar, which for some people would have made the condition
far worse.

The storm picked up during the early morning hours of Decem-

Captain Oates checks four of the ponies in their stable aboard the Terra Nova.

ber 2. Supplies on deck began to break loose as water washed over the lee rail. At times the men clung for their lives. Some tried to assist Oates and Dr. Edward Atkinson, one of the two surgeons, who worked throughout the day and night to keep the ponies standing up. The decks leaked in streams. In the engine room, Chief Stoker William Lashly stuck "gamely" to clearing the suction pumps despite being up to his neck in rushing water.

When the bilge pump choked to a dribble, the situation looked grim for the overloaded ship. The men formed a bucket brigade and, singing sea chanteys, kept bailing in shifts for the duration of the storm. Meares struggled to keep the dogs, which were tied up in the middle of the top deck, from being strangled by their chains. The force of the waves was so strong that one dog's chain snapped, washing the animal overboard. Unbelievably, the next wave washed

103

him back on deck again! It was thought this dog was Osman, a large black dog reputed to be king-dog because he was the leader and the most formidable fighter.

Two ponies, Davy and Jones, and one dog were dead when the gale finally abated, in addition to the loss of irreplaceable coal and oil. A third pony that had gone down and been put in a sling during the storm was back on its feet. On the following day, the beleaguered *Terra Nova* continued pitching heavily in turbulent seas, even though the weather had improved. Scott feared for the ponies under the forecastle. Although two appeared groggy and needed rest, Blucher seemed to suffer the most. The four in the midship stalls surprisingly fared better than those with more protection below.

The ponies slowly improved as the ocean swell diminished, although swollen legs irritated a few of the animals. Even Scott, the captain, had been disturbed by the motion of the ship and hadn't slept during the night. His thoughts flew to the "poor ponies" as he speculated how long the memory of such discomfort would remain with them. Who could tell? "But it would seem strangely merciful if nature should blot out these weeks of slow but inevitable torture."

The *Terra Nova* encountered the first pack ice and tabular icebergs sixty to eighty feet high on December 9. With the pack ice came a calm sea, giving the ponies the rest they so badly needed. Marveling at the scene, Scott stayed on deck until midnight when the sun dipped below the southern horizon. "The northern sky was gloriously rosy and reflected in the calm sea between the ice, which varied from burnished copper to salmon pink; bergs and pack to the north had a pale greenish hue with deep purple shadows, the sky shaded to saffron and pale green," he wrote.

During the twenty days of steaming slowly through the four hundred miles of pack ice, the men often went skiing when the ship was unable to move. The dogs that looked to be in the worst condition were taken on a sledge run at one point, and Meares reported they were very short of wind. Scott couldn't understand how they could get so fat when they were fed only two and a half biscuits a day.

The Terra Nova *in the ice pack*

The ponies, on the other hand, were looking well, especially those in the outside stalls.

But it was not always smooth sailing in the pack ice. Periodically, everyone on board was shaken up when the ship hit the ice in trying to force two floes apart or to break up one large chunk. This was especially true during the middle of the night when Bowers was on watch at the helm. Although he never damaged the ship, the collisions were so startling that Scott rushed up from his cabin to stop the determined young man.

One of the ponies went down in its stall on December 27 and was brought out on the open deck the next morning. "The poor beast is in a miserable condition," Scott wrote, "very thin, very weak on the hind legs, and suffering from a most irritating skin infection which is causing its hair to fall out in great quantities." Although Oates was unremitting in his care of them, Scott didn't think the Soldier realized the ponies could be exercised a little on deck while the ship was in the pack ice.

Completely frosted by a thin sheet of ice, the *Terra Nova* at last emerged south of the pack on December 30. But in the evening a blizzard met the expedition head on, pitching the ship once again. The ponies immediately began to feel the motion. Scott wondered "if fortune will ever turn her wheel."

On New Year's Eve they reached the Ross Sea, but not the end of their troubles. The wind and sea conditions continued to worsen. Although it could have endangered the ship, Scott steered into calmer water among the ice floes for the sake of the "wretched ponies." The clouds lifted at ten o'clock that night, revealing the majestic coastal mountains of Victoria Land radiating in the resplendent sun. Land ho!

Scott's first choice of a landing site at Cape Crozier, near the penguin rookeries on Ross Island, proved to be inaccessible, so the expedition sailed around the island to McMurdo Sound. (By this time Scott had abandoned his idea of establishing his main base at King Edward VII Land, although he intended to send a party to explore the region.) In McMurdo Sound, the *Terra Nova* was pre-

MASON

Glaciers gouge the coastal mountains of Victoria Land.

vented by a wall of ice from approaching Scott's first expedition quarters at Hut Point. He had to settle for a cape about fifteen miles north on Ross Island. Once the ship had moored at the edge of the sea ice, Scott, Dr. Wilson, and Lieutenant Evans crossed about a mile and a half of the ice to the beach. There they selected a position protected by low-lying hills for their station. Named for Evans, the cape was actually one of the spurs of Mount Erebus, and the "grand snowy peak with its smoking summit" towered above it.

After the arduous voyage, fortune finally treated the expedition "to the kindest smile" of calm weather and brilliant sunshine. To Scott this kind of weather, warm sun and invigorating cold air, was as close to perfection as anything he had ever experienced. At the same time, Herbert Ponting, the expedition photographer, was enraptured with the magnificence of the scene.

7 A Second Stables on Ross Island

WHILE Scott and his companions were ashore on January 4, 1911, the men on the *Terra Novà* began the week's work of unloading. Two of the tractors came off first, then the seventeen ponies. The men had great difficulty getting some of the ponies into the horse box, but Oates managed to persuade most of them. The others had to be lifted in by the sailors. All the ponies were thin and a few looked dragged down, but they were still full of vitality. As soon as the shaggy seventeen were picketed on the ice, they began to roll in the snow layer and whinny for joy. At last they were free to scratch the skin irritations from which they all suffered. They also helped each other by gnawing at their neighbors' itchy, sore flanks. Soon the beasts were "biting one another, kicking one another, and any one else, with the best will in the world," according to Cherry-Garrard. That hard-working young man was to become one of the most skillful pony handlers, in Scott's estimation, despite the necessity of seeing through glasses that caused him much inconvenience.

The ponies were taken ashore to a handy snow slope and tethered in a line where they couldn't eat any sand similar to that which had done in three of Shackleton's ponies. The dogs, meanwhile, began pulling loaded sledges across the ice to the shore,

One of the ponies is led out of the horse box onto the ice.

where the building party had erected a big green tent for temporary living quarters. Curious Adélies popped out of the water and waddled toward the dogs, which were frantic to get at them. Although the men tried to shoo the penguins away, nothing could stop the determined birds and blood soon stained the snow. On the next day, a half-dozen killer whales poked their snouts out of the water near the ice edge where two dogs were tied to one of the ship's mooring lines. When Ponting ran to photograph them, the cunning orcas dove and rose under the ice, breaking it into fragments. Ponting and the dogs were saved by the good luck that the ice didn't break directly beneath them. But that day killer whales earned a reputation for diabolical cunning that still persists.

After two days of rest, during which time the tractors were first used, the ponies began hauling loads from the ship to the shore where the framework of the hut was nearly up. Scott, Dr. Wilson, Dr. Atkinson, Bruce, and Cherry-Garrard each led a pony, changing to different ponies each time they returned to the ship for another load. Because Oates deemed two unfit and three untamed, only twelve of the ponies were put to work. But these performed admirably. Scott was amazed by their strength in pulling loads of seven hundred to a thousand pounds. He and his companions had expected the ponies to be helpless and exhausted after their horrendous voyage.

Although they started working well, the ponies soon began to get fidgety. The animals were annoyed by the crossbar and traces hanging behind their hocks and soon learned that the sledges would overrun them whenever they hesitated or stopped on the smooth ice. The more nervous ponies quickly became unmanageable. They would bite, kick, and run away without any warning. On one trip, Scott received a bump on the head and some scratches. A pony got away from Frank Debenham, one of the geologists, and galloped from the ship to the shore, where the load capsized before the pony and sledge dashed on to the building site. Oates, whom Scott credited with doing a crack job with the animals, "wisely" took the runaway straight back to the ship for another load.

It didn't take much of the ship-to-shore unloading to impress on

"The shaggy seventeen" picketed on the sea ice
SCOTT POLAR RESEARCH INSTITUTE

the expedition that the ponies were an "uneven lot." Punch and Nobby were steady workers. Blossom, Blucher, and Jehu apparently never recovered fully and were always weak animals. Several others were strong but impossible. One of these was soon known as Weary Willy. By his appearance he looked like a pony, but after a brief acquaintance Cherry-Garrard was convinced he was a cross between a pig and a mule. Weary Willy obviously was a strong animal. But since he always went as slowly as possible and stopped as often as possible, it was difficult for the young zoologist to form any opinion as to what load the beast was capable of pulling.

Although Weary Willy rarely moved faster than a trot, he proved his racing capacity one day when he had returned with his handler to the ship, after a trip during which the zoologist seemed to be pulling both the pony and the sledge. Suddenly one of the tractors backfired and Weary Willy started back across the ice at a pace that astonished Weary even more than his handler. The incident ended with Weary Willy's falling over the sledge and Cherry-Garrard. For days afterward, the young man felt like "a big black bruise."

But the two most difficult ponies were Christopher and Hackenschmidt. Christopher fought his handlers practically the entire time he was in Antarctica. He actually was a very dangerous animal. In Cherry-Garrard's view, Christopher "appeared to have come down to the Antarctic to initiate the well-behaved inhabitants into all the vices of civilization." It was doubtful whether even Oates could tame him. Hackenschmidt earned his name because of his vicious habit of using both fore and hind legs in attacking those who came near him. The reference seemingly points to George Hackenschmidt, the world's reigning freestyle wrestling champion at that time and one of the greatest wrestlers ever. However, George Hackenschmidt disliked the brutal tactics employed by many wrestlers and wasn't as vicious as the pony named after him.

The tractors and dogs, meanwhile, weren't pulling the loads expected of them. Sounding like threshing machines from a short distance, the tracked vehicles had a number of mechanical difficulties. Their performance was rather limited, causing Scott to fear the

Repairing one of the tractors, or motor sledges

machines would never pull the loads he had hoped. The dogs, still worn out from the voyage, were easily tired by hauling light loads in the hot sun, although on one occasion a team ran away, dragging for half a mile one of the dogs that had got turned over. Meares told the captain that several were suffering from snow blindness, but Scott was skeptical until Day, who had served on Shackleton's expedition, reminded him that Shackleton's dogs had been affected in the same way.

After each day's work, the huskies were staked out next to the ponies on the shore, near a nesting area for hundreds of skuas. Whenever disturbed, the birds would swoop down at the heads of the men, as though on a bombing run. One skua that was brooding a chick on a rock between the dogs and the ponies tried valiantly to drive off the intruders who were passing by every few minutes. The exhausted parent eventually was forced to give up the battle, and it settled down to the business of rearing its chick while Ponting tip-toed near for a photo.

The hut, meanwhile, neared completion. In addition to a double layer of dry seaweed in quilted sacks, Scott planned to insulate the

113

Scott's winter quarters at Cape Evans, with adjacent stables as they appear today

quarters, fifty by twenty-five feet in size, with pony fodder stacked all around it. On the northwest side, the stables were built by erecting an outer wall of bales six feet high a few yards from the hut wall. This was topped by a roof of rafters and tarpaulins. Finally, Bowers built a storeroom with packing cases and canvas on the southeast side.

As the condition of the ponies continued to improve, so did their free and wild spirits. On numerous occasions the little horses romped away, especially when they were being harnessed, but luckily neither they nor their handlers were injured. The ponies were particularly difficult to handle because they were led by halters without anything in their mouths. Metal bits would have been impossible for the ponies to endure in such cold weather. After chasing one pony after another, the men began to believe the condition of the "little devils" wasn't half as bad as they had imagined. The ponies even coped with stepping through spots in the melting sea ice.

But the deteriorating ice soon caused the expedition's first disaster. On January 8, the third tractor was unloaded from the ship. While being pulled across a slushy patch in the ice, it fell through, nearly taking one of the men with it. Another tractor and one of the ponies had pulled heavy loads across the same spot only the day before. It was a terrible blow for the polar enterprise that one of its vehicles, on which so much time and trouble had been spent, now lay at the bottom of the sea.

Scott and Meares marked a new route across the ice with kerosene cans, and the next day the unloading continued. Most of the pulling was done by the ponies, which seemed to like the new track. Three ponies, however, still hadn't been used at all, so in the evening Oates successfully led one of the nervous animals over the slippery surface with a load. Griffith Taylor, one of the geologists, had a more difficult time when he tried to lead another of the inexperienced ponies. With the expedition watching and laughing, the pony bolted away three times. Eventually Taylor arrived at the station with the obstreperous beast pulling his final load. Marching by, the geologist's face was set and he didn't say a word to anyone.

It was Taylor's turn to laugh the following evening when Oates decided to try leading the intractable animals, Christopher and Hackenschmidt, behind two of three loaded sledges during a transit to the station. Scott and another handler joined him. They made it safely to the shore, but while one of the sledges was being unpacked, Hackenschmidt suddenly became frightened and tore off with the sledge. He started for the other ponies, then finding the sledge still bumping behind him, galloped in widening circles over hills and boulders, narrowly missing Ponting and his camera. Finally, he dashed downhill to the camp. Although exhausted, Hackenschmidt was uninjured and little damage was done to the sledge. He immediately was hooked up again and the cavalcade started for the ship.

Halfway over the sea ice, the pony tied behind Scott's sledge became frightened when its leg got tangled in the lead rope. The animal tugged until it lifted the empty sledge, broke its halter, and dashed away. As the sledge banged to the ice, the pony in front snorted wildly and sprang forward. Scott managed to hold on until Oates rushed to help. The captain started again, but the frightened pony reared and plunged a second time, dumping Scott and charging off to the station. When the truant was caught at the campsite by Lieutenant Evans, it knocked the young officer over and romped away. Finally, Oates and Anton captured the beast and harnessed him to Evans' sledge. This unnamed animal reverted to its quiet, gritty nature during the return trip to the ship, where the sledges were loaded again. But on the way back to the station, the pony suddenly became fidgety. Evans called for Anton. Although both men tried to hold it, the pony bolted, upset the load, and galloped into camp with the empty sledge tailgating behind. The incident impressed on the shore party that the ponies were unpredictable and the handlers could never relax their guard.

The much admired Dr. Wilson tasted a similar experience when Chinaman (no relation to Shackleton's Chinaman) saw one of the strange tractors and took off with an empty sledge bumping behind him. Holding grimly onto the pony's chin strap, the doctor flew over the ice until Chinaman hit a slippery spot, sending them both sliding twenty yards into a heap. Wilson got to his feet first, still holding the pony's halter. Happily, neither was injured and afterward Chinaman "went like a lamb." The next ponies Wilson led handled more easily, especially one big one that had been named Uncle Bill after him. This pony and Victor, the two largest animals, were actually Siberian ponies, not Manchurian.

The landing of stores was completed by January 13, and the ponies began the task of hauling thirty tons of loose rock from the hillsides to the ship for use as ballast. Two days later, the expedition moved into its nearly finished hut and was "simply overwhelmed with its comfort," in Scott's words.

By today's standards, however, they had very few comforts. One item they did have was a Broadwood pianola, which during the last of the unloading was transported in pieces to the hut, reassembled, and tuned. The men gathered around it and sang "Home Sweet Home."

116

Petty Officer John Mather (of the ship's party) and his charge haul rocks for ballast on the Terra Nova.

While the men added final touches to the hut, the ponies rested and had time for their sores to heal. But they still had to be exercised daily and were taken on walks along the beach and in the vicinity of the hut. Scott, meanwhile, finalized plans for three exploratory missions. He would lead a party of men with dogs and eight ponies on a depot-laying journey across the Ross Ice Shelf to prepare for his trek to the Pole the following spring. After helping the depot crew get started, the *Terra Nova* would ferry a five-man team headed by Taylor across McMurdo Sound to geologize in the Victoria Land Mountains. The ship would then land Lieutenant Victor Campbell, five companions, and two ponies to explore King Edward VII Land before she sailed to New Zealand for the winter.

Oates wanted to take the weakest ponies on the depot-laying journey as far south as possible, then kill them and cache the meat for use by the dogs and the men on the trip to the Pole. But Scott was against this idea. Although the captain approved of using the animals to feed the men if need be, he was sentimental about killing them unnecessarily. Scott consequently picked a mixed bag when he chose the ponies for the depot-laying journey, including three of the strongest, Uncle Bill, Guts, and Punch. He assigned Punch to

117

Oates; Uncle Bill to Bowers; Guts to Cherry-Garrard; Weary Willy to Sub-Lieutenant Tryggve Gran, the Norwegian ski expert; Jimmy Pigg to Petty Officer Patrick Keohane; and Blucher to Petty Officer Robert Forde. Although Dr. Atkinson started out with Nobby, the pony was taken over by Scott soon after the party reached the ice shelf. At the same time, Lieutenant Evans took charge of Blossom from Thomas Crean. The ponies Jehu and Chinaman were tapped to accompany the Campbell party to King Edward VII Land.

Every pair of socks, every ounce of food had to be considered as the men calculated the loads to be hauled across the ice shelf. During the last two days before the depot party's departure, Oates was kept busy weighing out the pony food for the journey, sorting harnesses, and trying to manage his "most unruly mob." Scott worried about getting the animals past Glacier Tongue. As Shackleton had found, the glacier tip had to be crossed because it transected the only accessible route south on the sea ice remaining next to the shore of Ross Island.

On January 24, the ponies were carefully led over the rock and snow of Cape Evans, down onto South Bay, and then across about six miles of sea ice to Glacier Tongue. The *Terra Nova*, meanwhile, conveyed the dogs, sledges, and supplies to the first camp, located on the south side of the glacier. Why the ship didn't take the ponies, too, has never been explained. Perhaps Scott thought it would be more trouble loading and unloading them than walking them to the camp.

Bowers, who hadn't slept for seventy-two hours, was left momentarily at Cape Evans because he was still giving last-minute instructions about the management of the provisions while the depot party was away from the station. The diligent storekeeper then had to catch up with the party. In doing so, he nearly became lost while trying to follow them over what was unfamiliar terrain. Breathless, perspiring, and in great pain from banging his knee against a rock, Bowers started off being led by his pony, Uncle Bill. Apparently, Uncle Bill didn't want to be left behind. Nor did the pony appreciate what Bowers had done for him. The Marine lieutenant had

118

Emperor penguins seem to form a welcoming committee on the ice.

donned all his polar clothing so that Uncle Bill wouldn't have to carry the extra weight even though the pony was the biggest of the beasts.

It was precarious work getting the ponies across Glacier Tongue with its numerous shallow crevasses and holes. The men also had to be wary of the sea ice around the glacier because it was ready to break up and float out of McMurdo Sound to the ocean.

"If a pony falls into one of these holes I shall sit down and cry," Oates was heard to say. Three minutes later, Guts stepped in the middle of a snowed-over crack and sank to his stomach. Struggling in the brash ice and snow, the pony sank deeper and deeper until only his head and forelegs were visible above the slush. After much effort, the men managed to secure Guts with alpine ropes and haul out the trembling creature. The other ponies quickly were taken around the danger area. An hour later, according to Cherry-Garrard, Guts appeared to have forgotten the mishap and with the other ponies was pulling his first loaded sledge toward the Barrier.

Scott was pleased that the ponies worked with extraordinary steadiness, stepping out briskly as they followed in each other's tracks while pulling nine hundred pounds each. But this perfor-

119

MASON

Quarters built by Scott's Discovery *Expedition at Hut Point in 1902. McMurdo Station, center for present-day U.S. antarctic operations, is in the background.*

mance was short lived. The ponies soon began to sink and flounder in the snowy surface in which the men scarcely made an impression. It took them two days to reach the ice shelf, only about five miles from Hut Point. During this time, Jimmy Pigg strained a tendon and went lame. His leader, Patrick Keohane, encouraged him along, promising, "Come on, lad, you'll be getting to the Pole." Despite his strength, Uncle Bill was suffering with an old malady of weak forelegs, and Scott didn't expect him to last long. The men were anxious about both animals but they believed the two ponies would mend in time. To help protect them as well as the other ponies from chafing by the hard surface crust, their legs below the knee were wrapped with bandage-like putties.

In the afternoon of January 28, the depot party undramatically sledged up a short slope from the annual sea ice to the ice shelf. Only three of the thirteen men—Scott, Dr. Wilson, and Day—had been on the great Barrier before. The first loads were dumped about half a mile from the edge of the ice shelf at what was called Fodder Depot. The next morning, Jimmy Pigg rested while the other ponies made two trips to relay supplies from the last cache on the sea ice. When the party started this job, Oates let go of Punch's head for a moment and the spirited pony charged through the camp until his sledge hit another and broke. Punch galloped off, kicking furiously at the dangling traces behind him. When the pony had quieted down, Oates was able to retrieve him.

Tryggve Gran then tried to lead Weary Willy pulling a sledge. All went well as long as Gran skied alongside the normally lazy pony. But when he changed position and came up behind Weary Willy, the swish of the ski frightened Willy, who fled faster than his pursuer could keep up. This was the second and last time the pony was known to make any quick movement.

From Fodder Depot the supplies were taken on to a point about two miles from the Barrier edge, which the men called Safety Camp because they considered the site safe if the face of the ice shelf should break away, a frequent event. Scott received a great shock when the ponies began sinking very deep in the snow. It was a shock for the ponies, as well. They didn't seem to know what to do at first; then, braced for action, they would try to rush ahead. If the snow patch was small, the animals would arrive snorting and agitated on the harder surface. But if the soft area was extensive, they would struggle on until they were tired out. Most of them eventually began to plunge forward with both forefeet together in a series of jumps, jerking the sledge behind. Exhausted, they often had to stop. For Scott it was horrible to see them "half engulfed in the snow, panting and heaving from the strain." The ponies would fall sometimes and lie trembling, but they soon recovered their strength. The quieter, lazier ponies, surprisingly, had a much easier time of it.

The ponies obviously wouldn't last long under such conditions. Yet Shackleton somehow had gotten his animals a long way across the Barrier under similar circumstances. Scott held a war council

Pony snowshoes found at Cape Evans

and decided to try the bamboo and wire snowshoes that had been made especially for the ponies. To his dismay, he found that all except one set had been left behind at Cape Evans, despite the fact that the snowshoes "had been long and anxiously considered." Although Scott never said so, Oates was to blame. "The most loveable old pessimist" didn't have any faith in them.

But Scott was confident the party could double its daily mileage if the ponies had snowshoes. Taking the one set they had, the men tried to accustom the ponies one at a time to wearing the devices. When the set was put on Weary Willy, the result was "magical." Willy trotted around as though walking on hard ground. Scott consequently sent Meares and Dr. Wilson back with the dogs to fetch more snowshoes from the station at Cape Evans, twenty miles away. But the men returned the following day with the disheartening news that the bay ice had broken up and floated out to sea, preventing them from reaching the hut.

The depot party got underway again on February 2, leaving behind Dr. Atkinson who had been suffering with a painful heel

122

and Crean to care for him. Their ponies were turned over to Scott, who took charge of Nobby, and to Lieutenant Evans, who was given Blossom to lead. Despite the soft snow, most of the ponies made good progress. Only heavy Uncle Bill floundered where the others walked fairly easily. Bowers could do little to help the pony, which tried to go faster every time he was stymied. When Scott called for the one set of snowshoes, he was told Oates had left the devices behind at Safety Camp. He immediately sent Gran back on skis to retrieve them.

How to help the ponies posed a perplexing problem for the English leader. He suggested the animals might do better if they traveled at "night" when lower temperatures made the surface firmer even though the sun was still shining. The men agreed, and the cavalcade began its daily march about midnight, after sleeping during the day, which also permitted the ponies plenty of rest.

About 10:00 P.M. Scott would rouse the men, who would breakfast before feeding the ponies and breaking camp. With freezing fingers they would load the tents and camp equipment on the sledges, then remove the ponies' rugs, put on their harnesses, and fill their nose bags for the next halt. One by one the ponies would be taken off the picket line and yoked to a sledge. While the handlers held the ponies, the picket rope would be gathered up and loaded.

Sometimes there would be irritating delays when a group was late striking its tent or adjustments had to be made, such as to the putties. Fearful of keeping his nervous animal standing in the traces, Oates often would turn a wary eye on Christopher. When all was ready, Scott would shout, "All right, Bowers, go ahead," and the stocky lieutenant would lead off with Uncle Bill. At times, the ponies would have gotten cold and anxious while waiting, and when Scott gave the word to start they would charge ahead, with their drivers running and slipping after them.

The expedition eventually formed into a single column, marching through a vast stillness broken by the sounds of the ponies' plodding, the swish of the sledges, and the encouragements of the handlers. Then the patter of dog pads and directions shouted in Russian would be heard from behind.

Halfway through the daily march, about 3:30 A.M., the captain would take out his whistle and signal to Bowers, who would make a left turn before stopping. The picket line would be strung out and anchored by two sledges at either end. Then the ponies would be picketed and covered with their rugs, after which the dog teams were allowed to arrive in the camp. The men had "lunch" and the marching procedure started again about 5:00 A.M.

When the party camped for the day, the men had to build snow walls to protect the ponies on the picket line before crawling into sleeping bags. Scott's companions were dubious the first time they saw him dig crumbly blocks of snow and use them to construct a rough wall to the south of his pony. But the light wind, which persistently blows from the dome-shaped interior north to the sea, soon convinced them what a boon the walls could be. Every morning on camping, subsequently, each handler would begin to erect a wall behind his pony. After supper, he would complete the edifice, which meant losing the warmth temporarily gained from the hot hoosh and cocoa. But much to the men's chagrin, the matter didn't end there. The handler often would have to get out of his comfortable sleeping bag and rebuild the wall when his pony kicked it down. Weary Willy was particularly annoying in this respect. He would deliberately back into his wall and knock down the whole structure. But Guts was the worst offender. Cherry-Garrard had to put Guts's wall out of reach because it seemed to be the pony's aim in life to eat it, generally beginning at the bottom. The beast would dislodge a block and bring the entire shelter tumbling down.

More problems had to be dealt with during the march, particularly as a result of the Barrier surface. Approaching the party's fifth camp on February 3, for instance, Bowers and Uncle Bill suddenly plunged into a drift of deep snow. Weary Willy and Blossom were too close behind and followed. They struggled until they sank up to their bellies and couldn't move. Quickly, the wallowing animals were unharnessed and led with the other ponies from patch to patch

Protected by rugs and leg putties, four ponies stand behind a shelter wall of snow blocks at a camp.

until a firmer surface was found. While the exhausted men and animals camped for a rest, Gran returned with the only set of snowshoes, which at once were tried on Uncle Bill. The big pony was awkward for a few minutes, then settled down. Passing through places where the ponies had been thwarted by the surface, Bowers took Uncle Bill back and retrieved two of the sledges that had been left in the snow.

With Uncle Bill walking steadily on the snowshoes, the party pressed on the next evening. First the ponies had to cope with more fresh snow, then with crevasses. Oates, who had never peered down into a crevasse, asked one of the men what it was like and got the reply that it was "black as hell." Before long he nearly found out for himself when Punch got his legs into one of the cracks, then another, and finally sank bodily into a third. Luckily, the men pulled the pony out without much trouble. After the crevasse field, the ponies began to pull their loads easily on a hard, windswept surface. As a result they all were in good shape when the party camped; even Jimmy Pigg had recovered from his lameness. Here the men established Corner Camp depot, about thirty-five miles

125

from Hut Point, on the morning of February 4. They had been traveling for twelve days.

The dogs had been pulling well, but they, too, presented problems. Some were found to have been trained to attack strangers and they barked fiercely if anyone but their driver came near. While Scott was pointing out a stopping place to Meares, the dog Osman turned and nipped his leg slightly. Scott was convinced that if Meares hadn't been on the sledge the entire team, following the leader, would have been at him in an instant.

Like the ponies, the dogs seemed to be affected by the monotony of the journey. If they weren't eating or sleeping, they needed something interesting to do. While traveling, for example, they became so accustomed to the startling snap when the crust under their feet broke away that they used it to play a game. They would become alert at the sound and spring from side to side, as if hoping to catch the hidden creature responsible. To Scott, the dogs were almost human in their demand for "living interest," yet fatally less than human in their inability to foresee beyond their present situation. This distinction, along with their irrational, fierce instincts, resigned the English leader "to the sacrifice of animal life in the effort to advance such human projects as this." Still, it was a sacrifice he loathed to make.

8 On the Depot Trail

A blizzard at Corner Camp, the first encountered by the depot-laying party on the Barrier, immobilized the men in their tents for three long, unproductive days. They emerged into the "hell" outside only to feed the animals. Despite this care, Uncle Bill was said to have eaten one of his putties.

When the party proceeded on February 7, Scott discovered that the ponies had been more affected by the blizzard than anyone had realized. All were listless and several were visibly thinner than before, in addition to being still somewhat snow-blind. Most likely they hadn't slept during the gale-force storm. The worst case was Blucher, who looked like a scarecrow, earning him the nickname "Misery." Although the weight on his sledge was reduced to four hundred pounds, Misery collapsed during the second half of the night march. His load was reduced to two hundred pounds, but when this failed to help, Petty Officer Robert Forde ended up pulling the heavily laden sledge as well as leading the pony.

The blizzard and Misery's plight impressed on Scott that every care had to be taken to keep as many of the ponies alive as possible. In hopes they would perk up, he instructed Oates to give them extra amounts of food. Scott also decided the ponies' blankets would have to be improved before the journey to the Pole. The additional rations seemed to help, as well as a warmer sun during the day when the ponies rested after a cold night march. But the handlers agreed that the principal cause of the ponies' discomfort was the thinness of their coats, a problem Shackleton also had encountered. More than anyone realized, the ponies' coats must have been affected by transferring them from the Northern Hemisphere to the bottom of the world, where the seasons are reversed. Perhaps they should have been brought south two or three years in advance so that they could acclimatize.

The dogs, on the other hand, were in fine form. The storm had only been a rest for them. Curled snugly in the snow, they emerged from their hot, steaming holes only at mealtimes.

Unknown to Scott, the dogs of his rival Amundsen were being readied on the opposite side of the ice shelf for an enviable performance. Departing their base at the Bay of Whales on February 10, they covered about ninety miles in four days to reach 80°S., where the Norwegians depoted their first cache of provisions on the Barrier. On the outward trip Amundsen had hit on the novel idea of substituting dried fish for the black flags used to mark the route. His men stuck the fish on bamboo poles in the snow about every half-mile to break up the monotony for the dogs, and the eager huskies made the homeward journey in only two days. As a result, Amundsen accomplished Scott's depot goal at 80°S. in only six days, though he didn't have to travel as far inland to reach it. Because of the indentation of the coastline at the Bay of Whales, the Norwegian station, called Framheim, was located about sixty miles further south than Cape Evans.

The English, meanwhile, were battling across the ice shelf with their animals. As the weather became increasingly warmer, the ponies began stepping deeper into the softer snow. Lieutenant Evans' pony, Blossom, particularly had trouble walking due to his very small hooves and lagged behind in the column. Scott wondered what kind of snowshoes could be devised to help the ponies in such a situation. As it was, Evans had to drag Blossom over the final

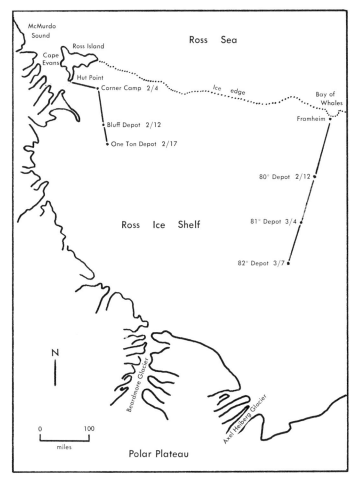

Map of Scott's and Amundsen's depot journeys during the first season's work

mile before the party camped on February 12 and built Bluff Depot, about ninety miles from Hut Point. There was also trouble with Osman, who was temporarily deposed as leader of the dogs because he was getting either "very disobedient or very deaf."

At Bluff Depot, Scott decided to reorganize. He sent Evans, Forde and Keohane back to Safety Camp with the weakest ponies, Blossom, Blucher, and Jimmy Pigg. Scott, Bowers, Cherry-

Garrard, Gran, and Oates continued to move south with the remaining five ponies; Dr. Wilson and Meares following with the two dog teams. Once again, fortune turned away from them. They were headed straight into a blizzard that left drifts of snow for the ponies to fight their way through. Gran's pony, Weary Willy, dropped so far behind that the dogs caught up with him. Suddenly, Weary Willy fell and the dogs lunged for him. Fighting gallantly, the pony bit and shook some of the huskies with his teeth while Gran and Meares rushed in, breaking their dog sticks in an effort to protect Willy. When the dogs had been beaten off, Gran unharnessed the badly bitten pony and led him on without the sledge, which was picked up later. Willy arrived at camp covered with blood and looking very sick.

The party attempted to continue but Willy's condition forced them to stop after less than a mile. Trying to help the little horse recover, they gave him a feed of hot bran, built a large snow wall beside him, and put some extra sacking around him to keep him quiet and warm. The extra care seemed to help, and Willy was better the next day.

But the weak ponies in Evans' group that had been sent back from Bluff Depot weren't as fortunate. Evans and his group had traveled only four miles when they encountered the same blizzard that struck Scott's party. Blucher, being led by Petty Officer Forde, was in no condition to withstand the storm. The sailor spent hours trying to keep the pony alive by feeding him and walking him around. Despite Forde's efforts, Blucher fell and couldn't get up. Then all the men tried to get the poor creature on his feet, but he couldn't stand and died soon after.

When the blizzard was over, Evans' contingent marched on ten miles before Blossom forced a halt. The pony could barely move, stopping with his legs outstretched and nose to the surface. Although the men rested him, fed him, and covered him with rugs, Blossom had become emaciated and shriveled up as a result of the storm. So he, too, died and was left there on the depot trail. Both Blossom and Blucher had been the oldest ponies and the two Oates thought the least of. Their loss, nonetheless, was another setback for the unlucky expedition.

Meanwhile, Scott's ponies were in trouble. Breaking through a thin hard crust on the surface, they sank deep into the snow underneath. Big Uncle Bill for the first time refused at intervals to move. Scott was forced to stop several times and wait while the ponies rested. If only they had some kind of snowshoes that worked!

A cold wind and a temperature of $-21°$ F. helped the ponies in Scott's group on the following night's march by hardening the surface, although it meant frostbitten ears, noses, and cheeks for the men. Despite the improved surface, the exhausted ponies were failing and couldn't go much farther, forcing an end to the depot journey. In Cherry-Garrard's opinion, the expedition had much to learn about using ponies on the Barrier. The animals had become thin and very hungry. Their rations were inadequate for the conditions on the ice shelf, and the autumn temperatures and winds were too much for their strength.

Scott consequently had to establish the last preliminary depot on February 15, about 150 miles south of Hut Point and a crucial 36 miles short of his goal for that all-important cache at 80°S. More than a ton of provisions were stored here at what was called One Ton Depot, Scott's largest supply point on his route to the Pole. But now he would have to travel farther back from the Pole to reach it—a total of 730 miles. Little did he realize what those extra 36 miles would cost him the following year.

With Osman restored to leadership of one team, Scott took the dogs and dashed ahead with Meares, Dr. Wilson, and Cherry-Garrard. He was anxious for news of Campbell's exploration attempt of King Edward VII Land, in addition to concern for Dr. Atkinson and Crean who had been left behind at Safety Camp, the second of the five depots made on the ice shelf. The other four members of Scott's party and the five ponies followed the dog teams at a slower pace, with Bowers and Uncle Bill steering the way as before.

Although all of the ponies were in poor shape, Weary Willy was the worst. He was tied to another pony (unnamed) and literally made to jump along as the other pony pulled the sledge. After accomplishing only ten and a half miles, Bowers and his companions were forced to camp on February 19 because Willy refused to go another inch. Pathetic Willy was given an extra ration of oats at the expense of the other ponies in an effort to try to help him. Uncle Bill, however, wasn't about to accept the shortage of food, especially since he was bigger and had worked harder in leading the column. With his tethered leg Uncle Bill pulled toward him one of the sledges, which were now too light to anchor the animals properly. He then forced his nose into the men's precious biscuit container and "helped himself liberally" in Bowers' words.

Racing ahead of Bowers' contingent, Scott was nearing Safety Camp on February 21 about midnight when he decided to take a shortcut instead of following the outward route. In the dim light Scott and Meares suddenly saw the middle dogs of their team disappear into a crevasse. Fortunately Osman, although nearly choking to death, used his extraordinary strength to hang on to the far edge. Scott and Meares leaped from the sledge, miraculously saved by a snowbridge. They quickly pulled the sledge clear and anchored it. Peering over the rim of the abyss, they could barely see the howling dogs suspended in all sorts of terrifying positions. One dog was trying frantically to claw its way up the wall of the crevasse, while two suspended in midair bit and fought whenever they swung together. Two others had dropped out of their harness and landed on a second snowbridge farther below.

Dr. Wilson and Cherry-Garrard rushed to help, and the men hurriedly unloaded their irreplaceable equipment from the sledge. After cutting Osman out of his harness, they ran the sledge across the gap and, working from it, managed in about an hour to haul up eleven of the dogs. Scott couldn't leave the remaining pair on the snowbridge below and ordered his men to lower him sixty-five feet down to the huskies, where he found them coiled up and asleep!

After the last pair was pulled to safety, the dangling Scott heard a din of shouts and barking above. Then the rope handlers abruptly disappeared. Bewildered, he hung inside the crevasse until the other men managed to separate the two dog teams, which had gotten into a fight, and return for him. Happily, not one dog was seriously injured during the episode, and Osman's reputation was cemented for the rest of his life.

Scott's band reached Safety Camp the next day, February 22, and found Evans' party with only one pony, Jimmy Pigg. Dr. Atkinson and Crean, who had been left there at the beginning of the journey, had gone to Hut Point to pick up the mail. When Scott eventually opened his long-awaited letter from Campbell, the news was shattering. Campbell's party, during its unsuccessful attempt to land at King Edward VII Land, had found Amundsen camped at the Bay of Whales, sixty miles closer to the Pole than Scott's headquarters at Cape Evans! Scott, it will be recalled, had assumed the Norwegian would make his bid from the opposite side of the continent. Amundsen had better equipment and 116 Greenland huskies, chosen by experts and well trained. He had also selected men who thoroughly understood dogs and were accomplished

The Terra Nova *arrives at the Bay of Whales to find the Norwegian expedition.*

Giving whisky to one of the two ponies swum ashore from the Terra Nova

skiers and knowledgeable of ice terrain. The Norwegian was convinced that Scott's and Shackleton's mistrust of dogs was ill con-
ceived. Amundsen planned to use his dogs to make storage depots
south across the ice shelf. He did not want his trip to the Pole the
next season to be slowed down by hauling a large amount of supplies, which was what happened to Shackleton and Scott due to
their reliance on the ponies and motors.

When Campbell returned to Cape Evans after meeting Amundsen, the two ponies taken on the *Terra Nova* had to be swum ashore
because the sea ice had broken up in the area. Chinaman and Jehu
were lowered in the sling and, with the sailors using the lead ropes

to hold up their heads, the ponies were towed through the icy water by one of the whaleboats. Chinaman swam vigorously but Jehu seemed to be paralyzed and passively submitted to being hauled through the mile of freezing sea. At the station, they were each given half a bottle of whisky and rubbed down to restore their circulation. One of the two became "quite intoxicated" and behaved in "a very laughable and eccentric manner but he soon shook off the effects of the debauch." Which pony wasn't specified, but Jehu was severely weakened by the trauma of swimming ashore and nearly died. (Coincidentally, Shackleton's Chinaman had also taken a plunge in McMurdo Sound while being landed there in February of 1908.)

Scott had a trauma to deal with, too, since Amundsen had arrived on the scene. But the captain was not about to be panicked, although he realized that the Norwegians could start their journey to the Pole early the next spring, which he couldn't do because the ponies would be destroyed by the cold weather at that time of the year. Scott decided the wisest course of action was to proceed exactly according to his plans, which included a third season of exploration using seven Himalayan mules, in addition to the dogs, which he requested in a letter sent to New Zealand on the *Terra Nova*. The leader had discussed the situation with Oates who thought trained Indian transport mules would do better than ponies in the Antarctic. Oates expected the mules to be less troublesome and have a more uniform walking pace.

After a two-day blizzard had ravaged the ponies, all the depot-laying contingents joined up at Safety Camp on February 27. The storm had buried the ponies up to their bellies behind their shelter walls, leaving them terribly emaciated, particularly Weary Willy, who was in pitiable condition. Because of the bad weather and cold, Scott decided to move on quickly to Hut Point. He sent the two dog teams on their way, then the ponies. Uncle Bill was ready first, and Bowers started with him. Punch, Nobby, Guts, and Willy were harnessed next. But when Willy was led forward, he fell. Scott had to regroup. He sent Crean and Cherry-Garrard ahead with the

135

three other ponies in Willy's bunch to join Bowers, who had gone over the edge of the Barrier and was waiting at the bottom of a snow incline on the sea ice. Oates and Gran stayed behind at Safety Camp to help Scott's desperate efforts to save Willy.

The men got the poor creature up and fixed him a hot oat mash. After waiting an hour, Oates tried to make a start with Willy, but the ailing pony marched only five hundred yards before falling again. The men camped, built a snow wall around Willy, and tried to get him on his legs. Despite his pitiful struggles, Willy couldn't get up again. All the men could do was to prop him up before they turned in. During the night, Willy's long battle finally came to an end, only seven miles from shelter at Hut Point. His death emphasized the terrible effect of blizzards on the ponies. Although their coats were thin, Scott believed that the little horses would lose condition easily even with the best coat in such snowstorms.

Crean and Cherry-Garrard with their three ponies, meantime, had joined Bowers on the sea ice. Although they were unable to follow the dog teams, which had dashed off leaving them behind, the three men pushed on, stopping frequently because of the ponies' weakened condition and a black mist that limited visibility. Before long, Bowers detected the ice moving around them and started back. They trekked as far as the exhausted ponies would drag the loaded sledges and camped where Bowers thought it would be safe. Once they had built walls to protect the ponies and fed them, the intrepid explorers retired after midnight to their tent to fix a meal for themselves. It was so dark that curry power was used for cocoa and Crean drank his down before discovering the mistake. He undoubtedly had little trouble keeping warm that night.

Hearing a noise about 4:30 A.M., Bowers got up, thinking, "My pony is at the oats!" But when he stomped outside in his socks, the indomitable Marine discovered their little camp was on a chuck of ice heaving up and down with the swell of the sea. "Cherry, Crean, we're floating out to sea!" he shouted. The ice had split under the picket line, cutting Guts's wall of snow in half. Guts had disappeared into a dark streak of water.

Bowers leapt to the next ice floe to rescue one of the sledges used to anchor the picket line and managed to drag it back as the ice around the tent broke in two. The men and three ponies luckily were all safe and together. Bowers, who never considered abandoning anything, paused to put on his boots, remarking that they had been in a few tight places before, but this was about the limit, even for him.

The men packed up camp and harnessed the ponies in record time. They found that Punch would jump the wide cracks and the other two ponies would follow him. In this manner they progressed slowly, returning from each new floe to retrieve the four sledges. They often had to wait for leads in the ice to close so they could cross; at other times they had to detour. During one wait, the practical Cherry-Garrard distributed chocolate and biscuits. Bowers didn't want to think about food at such a time, but in half an hour he had eaten all of his share.

After jumping from one floe to another in "great style," the ponies were left chewing each other's head ropes and harnesses each time the men returned for the sledges. "Their implicit trust in us was touching to behold," Bowers wrote. As the party neared the Barrier, the sea around them was like a cauldron with killer whales hunting for seals. The orcas, their large black fins making them

A killer whale, or orca, lurks among the ice floes.

U.S. NAVY

look like sharks, were blowing with a "terrific roar." Six hours later, the men worked their way with the ponies to a thick piece of ice in a line of loose floes floating along the Barrier's cliff-like face. They could have used one of the twelve-foot sledges as a ladder to climb the ice shelf, which was about twenty feet high at that point, but they decided to stay with the ponies. Someone had to try to reach Scott by jumping across the floes, and Crean volunteered to go. Fortunately, the weather had cleared somewhat, the swell had diminished, and the light was improving as Crean negotiated the treacherous ice; hours later he reached safety on the Barrier near where Scott was camped.

Bowers and Cherry-Garrard spent an anxious day on their ice floe, waiting and hoping a wind from the south wouldn't send them off to sea. They fed the ponies all they could eat while orcas with huge black and white heads and "sickening pig eyes" bobbed up and down a few yards away from them. Skua gulls, picturing them as certain carrion, settled down nearby to wait.

Once Crean, exhausted and nearly incoherent, managed to relate what had happened, Scott marched to the rescue. He was very angry at Bowers for not abandoning all and deeply worried because Bowers and Cherry-Garrard had virtually no experience with sea ice in such a situation. When his party reached them, Scott was relieved that the two young men were all right. But Bowers was more concerned about the ponies, asking, "What about the ponies and the sledges?"

"I don't care a damn about the ponies and sledges," Scott shouted down to him. "It's you I want, and I am going to see you safe here up on the Barrier before I do anything else."

A rope was tossed to Bowers and Cherry-Garrard, and they were pulled up to safety. "My dear chaps, you can't think how glad I am to see you safe," Scott greeted them. But Bowers was determined not to give up and persuaded Scott to let them return while Oates tried digging a slope to get the animals up. Suddenly, the ice began to move and Scott ordered them back. Bowers ran and took the nose bags off the ponies and with Cherry-Garrard's help hauled up

138

Dr. Wilson's sketch, "The rescue from the sea ice, March 1, 1911"

the sledges just as a lane of black water widened to seventy feet between the nearest ice floe and the Barrier.

Since it was hopeless to try to rescue the ponies at this point, the men retreated half a mile from the edge and pitched what they called Rescue Camp. Scott and Bowers returned while supper was cooking and found killer whales tearing up and down like race-horses in the channel between the ice floes and the Barrier. The ponies were sailing away parallel to the ice shelf. Bowers tried to cheer up his captain by reminding him that ten ponies remained for their transport to the Pole, but Scott was gloomy. The best of those beasts were about to be lost.

When the other men turned in after dinner, Bowers walked back to the Barrier edge once again and followed it about a mile until he came abreast of the stranded ponies. "Poor trustful creatures!" he called them. They didn't seem disturbed or doubtful that the men

139

would bring them their breakfast nose bags as usual in the morning. "If I could have done it then, I would gladly have killed them rather than picture them starving on that floe out on the Ross Sea, or eaten by the exultant Killers that cruised all around."

In the morning Bowers scanned the ice floes with binoculars until he spotted the green horse rugs. He quickly brought the other men to the rescue. Scott agreed to let them try to save the ponies only if they would run for safety when he called. Taking Oates and Cherry-Garrard with him, Bowers picked a route down the Barrier face and across six floes. When they reached the animals, the men tried to jump Punch over the first gap, but the pony balked and plunged into the freezing sea. Punch couldn't be pulled out, and Oates was forced to use a pickax to end the animal's suffering.

Scott called to the men and pointed out a better route across the ice. Following his captain's directions, Bowers tried repeatedly to get Nobby across to the next floe. The pony, however, wouldn't budge. Scott ordered the men to kill the ponies, but this time Bowers pretended not to hear. Bowers tried once more and succeeded in getting Nobby to make the jump. Seizing the opportunity, Oates followed quickly with Uncle Bill.

Leaving the ponies temporarily, the men worked their way along the ice shelf until they found a low point to get the animals up. Scott and Cherry-Garrard started digging a slope while Bowers and Oates returned for the ponies with a sledge that they could use as a bridge if necessary. Crean, who had become snow-blind, stood by unable to help.

The new route proved to be much easier, and the two men brought the ponies back close to the ice shelf. Scott rushed Nobby up to safety and handed him over to Crean to hold. When Uncle Bill was being coaxed to leap from the final floe, however, a group of killer whales burst out of the water. "Good God, look at the whales!" someone shouted. Turning around, the men on the floe were greeted by twelve menacing orcas facing them in a straight line. In front of this rank rose another killer whale like a captain before his troops. Frightened, Uncle Bill jumped sideways and

140

missed the floe with his hind legs. The men managed to get the pony to the Barrier edge by pulling him, partly submerged, through thin ice. For some unknown reason, the whales didn't dive under the ice and attack the pony.

Scott wanted the men to leave the animal, but again Bowers pretended not to hear. Getting onto a patch of brash ice that had frozen together, he fastened a rope to each of Uncle Bill's forelegs. The men pulled until they got the horse up onto the brash ice. Cold and in shock, the poor creature lay helplessly on his side.

"He's done; we shall never get him up alive," Oates said as Bowers, sick with disappointment, tried in vain to get the pony on his feet. Three times Uncle Bill struggled and fell back. Then a large chunk of the Barrier began to break away, and Scott demanded the men return. But Bowers and Oates remained with the suffering animal.

"I can't leave him to be eaten alive by those whales," Bowers insisted.

Oates was just as reluctant. "I shall be sick if I have to kill another horse like I did the last," he said.

Left with no other choice, Bowers followed Oates's directions and wielded his pickax. He didn't want anyone but himself to kill his pony. Carrying the blood-stained pickax instead of leading Uncle Bill, Bowers at last jumped with Oates to the face of the Barrier.

The loss of three more ponies, Guts, Punch, and Uncle Bill, was another example of the bad luck that Scott's expedition encountered. Only six hours before the ponies had become trapped on the sea ice they could have walked easily across the frozen sound to Hut Point. As a result of this and the other setbacks during the depot-laying, the English leader began to doubt his expedition's chances of reaching the Pole. Neither the tractors, the dogs, nor the ponies had worked out. He would have been even more depressed if he had known how well the Norwegians were doing a few hundred miles on the other side of the ice shelf. As Scott's party marched along the Barrier to Ross Island, Amundsen was establishing his

Dr. Wilson holds Nobby.

second depot, located at 81°S., 160 miles from his station, Framheim. It held half a ton of provisions.

On March 4, Scott's party with Nobby was met on the slopes of Ross Island by Evans' group with Jimmy Pigg, and the two ponies were reunited after many weeks. As a welcome, Jimmy Pigg bit Nobby on the back of the neck! The ponies were eventually guided over six miles of hilly terrain to Hut Point, where the two survivors of the eight ponies that had started on the depot journey at last enjoyed comfortable quarters under the veranda of the *Discovery* hut.

The day after Scott's party returned to Hut Point (March 7), Amundsen and his dog teams cached another half ton of provisions on the Barrier, then headed back to base. This, the Norwegian's third depot, was located at 82°S., 230 miles south of Framheim.

Scott was forced to wait a month at Hut Point for the sea to freeze and enable his men to reach their winter quarters at Cape

142

Petty Officer Patrick Keohane and Jimmy Pigg

Evans, fifteen miles away. On April 11, Scott with eight companions decided to start for Cape Evans, leaving the others to bring the animals when thicker ice made the journey safer. Two days later, Scott's band startled Ponting, who was outdoors taking photos. Seeing them coming over the slopes, Ponting thought they were the Norwegians because they looked like "ruffians." They hadn't been able to bathe in nearly three months.

The homecoming was joyous until it was learned that one of the dogs and Hackenschmidt had died during the depot journey. Edward Nelson, the expedition's biologist, had performed a post-mortem but couldn't find any reason for the pony's death. Despite the best care, Hackenschmidt had gradually sickened until he was too weak to stand and had to be put out of his misery. Anton believed the pony had died out of pure "cussedness" in his determination not to do any work on the expedition. Scott agreed that Hackenschmidt had always been very difficult and probably would

143

have been a continuing source of trouble to them. Such considerations helped to soften the news of his death.

On the brighter side, Scott was pleased to see the improvements the men had made to the hut and their equipment during his absence. Anton, with the help of Lashly, had completed furnishing the stables. They had built neat stalls the entire length of the shelter with side boards and with tin sheeting on the front wall to defeat the "cribbers," ponies fond of biting the wall boards. Scott regretfully told them that some of the stalls would no longer be needed, and some later were removed so that all but two or three of the ponies could enjoy more space with room to lie down.

The eight ponies at Cape Evans looked fit despite the meager diet they had been kept on. Scott found their coats surprisingly long and "woolly" in contrast to those of Nobby and Jimmy Pigg, who had had less fatty food to eat. Anton, Lashly, and Demetri, as well as F. J. Hooper, the steward, and Thomas Clissold, the cook, had been exercising the unused ponies, mostly by riding them bareback along the boulder-strewn beach, up the slope to Skua Lake, and back down to the hut. Scott, however, wasn't pleased when he first saw the riders charging over the slopes on the ponies. "There were many incidents in which horse and rider parted with abrupt lack of ceremony," he commented. He felt this wasn't the best form of exercise for the animals, even though the men were having a great time. But he decided not to say anything and left it to Oates to put the damper on the fun. Bowers, meanwhile, sought out Victor, the other Siberian pony, and claimed him for his own, provided that Scott approved.

As the sun set for the winter, casting its rosy rays across the white mountains, ice, and the dark sea, the men and animals still at Hut Point continued waiting for the sea ice to thicken. Scott was very anxious about them. Meanwhile, the captain instituted night-watchman duty, as Shackleton had done, and took the inaugural watch himself. The task involved looking after the fire in the hut and the animals, and making scientific observations of the brilliant displays of the aurora in the night sky.

144

On May 13, the party from Hut Point finally arrived with the dogs, Nobby, and Jimmy Pigg. Scott was greatly relieved to have them back safely, writing that "everything seems to depend on these animals." Despite his experience with them on the Barrier, he still considered the ponies his most reliable source of transport across the ice shelf.

9 Winter at Cape Evans

DURING the winter at Cape Evans, Scott and his twenty-seven companions were kept busy with a number of scientific experiments, equipment to ready, and plans to make for the spring sledging. Sixteen of this group Scott would select to accompany him on the trip to the Pole. Lectures were given regularly, among other activities, to inform the men as well as entertain them. Although everyone spoke on his speciality, the men particularly looked forward to Oates's talks on horse management because he was shy and known not to be a speaker. But he surprised them all with an elaborate discourse, which included his plans to feed the ponies frequent light meals during the winter to conform to their natural grazing habits. In the spring he would give them cold food and increase their exercising hours to harden them for the summer sledge hauling.

The ponies' winter routine, consequently, began with a feeding of chaff every morning. Between breakfast and lunch they were exercised by their handlers when blizzards allowed. Whether the task was pleasant or difficult for the men depended on the pony and the weather. The change in temperature between the warm stables and outdoors was another problem. The ponies weren't eager to be led into the chill. Once on the cold, dark, windy sea ice, they would try

Lieutenant Edward Evans (left) *and Petty Officer Crean exercise two ponies during the winter.*

to shake off their handlers and gallop back to the hut, where they would dodge their pursuers until they tired of the game. Then they would walk quietly into the stables on their own. Inside, they were welcomed by the "triumphant squeals and kickings of their companions."

According to Cherry-Garrard, the worst days were those when it was difficult to determine whether or not the ponies should be taken on the sea ice. If the sky was overcast, the handlers might lose their bearings and become lost. Or a blizzard might break, suddenly trapping them. Generally, the risk was taken because the men considered it better to be a little overbold than overcautious. They were also lured by the thrill involved.

On one typical occasion when the young zoologist and Bowers decided to take the ponies out, it was snowing lightly without the moon, stars, or even a light breeze to indicate the direction. The

147

daring men took their steeds as far as the tall cliffs of the Barne Glacier, then turned toward a small tide crack in the middle of a nearby bay where a thermometer screen had been placed. After reading the temperature by the light of a match, they started back toward the hut. But in fifteen minutes they realized they were lost. Fortunately, they encountered a familiar iceberg and determined that they had been walking at right angles to the route home.

Bowers started exercising Victor by riding him, apparently unknown to Scott. One day when the pony dumped him in a tide crack, he said to his friend Cherry-Garrard, "I'll soon get used to him." In a subdued tone he added, "To say nothing of his getting used to me."

Following the morning exercise, the ponies were given snow for its water content, then chaff and either oats or oil cake on alternate days. Portions were determined by the work that the little horses were able to do during the winter or were expected to do in the future. Once the ponies were fed, the men sat down to lunch.

At five o'clock in the evening the ponies were given snow, hot bran mashed with oil cake or boiled oats and chaff, and, finally, a small quantity of hay. Oates was dubious about the chaff, made of young wheat and hay. There didn't seem to be any grain in it. But he believed it would serve as food during the winter when the ponies were fairly inactive and required less nourishment. His opinion, however, proved to be too hopeful, according to Cherry-Garrard. Most of the ponies were skin and bones by the end of the winter, although Scott gives the impression that the majority were in good shape.

The bran, on the other hand, seemed good for the ponies because it forced them to chew the oats mixed with it, which meant they digested it better. Two types of oats had been brought for them: brown and white. Although the Soldier considered both good for producing work, the white oats seemed a better quality. The oil cake also gave the animals lots of energy.

Oates emphasized the value of training the ponies so they could pull with less effort, although he realized training was difficult when the handlers were mostly walking the horses for exercise. He hoped that some training could be done by walking the ponies fast and occasionally making them step backward. But little training was actually accomplished with the headstrong beasts.

In addition to being in charge of all the ponies, Oates took the troublesome Christopher as his horse to handle. Christopher, who had established himself as a devil during the unloading of the *Terra Nova*, hadn't changed his ways. He was considered "really savage" and a "man-eater." Cherry-Garrard believed that Oates's patience and tact with this dangerous beast might prove to be a model for any administrator of a lunatic asylum. Oates had the additional task of designing new rugs to cover the ponies' hindquarters, a decision Scott had made during the depot-laying.

The ponies caused few serious problems during the winter, although there were anxious moments such as when Jimmy Pigg managed to get himself twisted up while his head was tied to the stanchions on either side of his stall. Fortunately Oates heard him and, after quickly cutting his head ropes, got the frightened pony on his feet again. Then Jimmy Pigg had an attack of colic, a serious pain in the digestive tract. Oates took the bad-luck pony from the stables out to the sea ice where he doctored him. By evening,

Feeding time in the stables

ALEXANDER TURNBULL LIBRARY

Jimmy Pigg was eating again, and he recovered the next day.

All of the ponies developed an annoying skin irritation, which caused several of them to rub off patches of hair, something they couldn't afford in such a climate. Oates believed their feed was responsible and changed it, but Scott felt sure it was due to some parasite. He was right. A tiny body louse was captured from Snatcher's coat and identified under Dr. Atkinson's microscope. A dilute solution of carbolic acid was then used to rid the ponies of their pests, until the expedition ran out of the chemical. Relying on his experience with troop horses, Oates steeped tobacco in water and used it to wash the ponies. His simple remedy soon got rid of the bothersome lice. Although such parasites are found on seals and penguins, most likely the ponies brought the pests with them.

A week after they celebrated Midwinter's Day on June 22, Dr. Wilson, Bowers, and Cherry-Garrard made their famous trek across Ross Island to study the Emperor penguins at Cape Crozier. The unusual birds had never been observed during the winter when they rear their young. Unknowingly, the explorers picked a five-week period of persistent blizzards and fierce cold. It took them nineteen days to cover the hazardous, 67-mile route. After surviving a blizzard while camped above the rookery, they grappled their way back, cuddling three penguin eggs that later were used to prove penguins were related to flying birds.

Their report of temperatures continuously below −60° F. on the other side of the island led Scott to wonder if Amundsen, camped 350 miles west, was experiencing a bad winter and having trouble keeping his dogs alive. To the contrary, the Greenland huskies were in good shape.

While the Cape Crozier trio were away, one of the best ponies, Bones, abruptly stopped eating and was distressed for no apparent reason. Oates diagnosed the problem as colic. No one was particularly concerned at first because Jimmy Pigg had recovered speedily under similar circumstances. When Crean took Bones out for exercise, however, the pony was seized with spasms of pain every few minutes. He first dashed forward as though to escape it, then tried

Held by Petty Officer Crean, Bones stands harnessed to a sledge with his New Zealand horse rug pushed up on his withers.

to lie down with Crean laboring to keep the strong little beast on his legs.

Bones was much worse when he returned to the stables, where Oates and Anton tried to ease his misery by dragging a warm sack against the underside of his belly. After Bones repeatedly tried to lie down, Oates decided it was wiser to let him. Bones stretched out at full length, occasionally twitching horribly with pain and raising his head with a patient, pleading expression on his face. When the pain became intense, he scrambled to his feet. But strangely he didn't utter a sound. Hours later, the men finally decided Bones was dangerously ill. Oates gave him two opium pills, and sacks heated in the hut oven were placed on him. Oates and Crean stayed by the pony's side throughout the night, and Scott stopped in from time to time to check on the patient.

At midnight, after twelve hours of pain, Bones began to improve. While still lying on his side, his spasms stopped. His eye looked less

151

distressed and his ear began to prick up at any noise. When Scott visited the stable about 2:30 A.M., Bones suddenly raised his head and got up on his legs, as though making a heroic effort for his captain. He began to nose at some hay and to poke his neighbor, a sure sign that he was getting better.

The men found the cause of Bones's trouble the next day: a small ball of semifermented hay covered with mucus and tapeworms. Attached to this was a piece of the lining of the pony's intestine. Dr. Atkinson expertly examined the parasite sample and announced the problem wasn't too serious if care was taken in feeding the ponies for a week.

After some discussion, the men decided the contributing causes were the fermentation of the hay, insufficient water, overheated stables, and a chill from being exercised following a recent gale. Scott consequently gave instructions that the stove should be used more sparingly in the stables and a hole cut for ventilation nearby. An allowance of water was added to the ponies' snow ration and feeding was watched carefully.

Oates reported the following day that a few of the other ponies appeared to have worms, and he and Scott began considering remedies. To their alarm, Chinaman stopped feeding and went down in his stall the next morning. But in only half an hour he was up and apparently well once more.

The ponies soon recovered and returned to being unpredictable. Chinaman developed a habit of squealing and kicking the stable, whereas Nobby kicked harder without squealing until he succeeded in knocking down part of his stall. On the other side of the hut wall, the sleepless men imagined dreadful things were happening to the poor ponies. But when the night watchman investigated, the little devils blinked at him "with a sleepy air as though the disturbance could not possibly have been there!" Anton theorized that Chinaman kicked and squealed at night to keep himself warm.

When Bones began hammering away merrily at the back of his stall for no apparent reason, the men decided something had to be done and covered the boards with several layers of sacking. Scott says their primary concern was that the ponies might injure themselves. Yet one wonders if the sleepless explorers would have been sad if Chinaman, Nobby, and Bones had gone temporarily lame at night.

But there were often moments of comedy with the ponies, too. Chinaman, for instance, always took too large a mouthful of snow and suffered the consequences, shuffling around with a pained expression while the snow chilled his insides. As soon as the snow melted, he would gobble another mouthful. He seemed unable or unwilling to follow the example of the other ponies, who either took smaller bites or, screwing up their faces like children forced to eat vegetables, melted large portions of snow on their tongues before swallowing it.

Victor and Snippets became addicted to wind sucking. They continually sucked air while biting into the manger board of their stalls. When the board was removed at feeding time, they would search in vain for something to anchor onto with their teeth in order to start sucking wind. Snippets later established a new record for eating almost anything when Oates found him devouring seal blubber. These two windsuckers were blamed for the sharp nips the men felt in the near darkness as they walked down the narrow passage between the stalls.

Despite the great difficulties with the ponies, they and their handlers were "on the best of terms," except for Christopher. Most of the handlers were sailors who possessed a profound love for animals, as demonstrated on the *Terra Nova* when it left New Zealand. The little horses were treated as friends and companions rather than as beasts of burden. Unlike the way they had been handled in their Manchurian homeland, the ponies were never hit by the Englishmen. They also lived better than they had before. But the men weren't blind to the ponies' vices or their limited capacity for thinking. In Cherry-Garrard's opinion, the ponies rivaled English politicians in having "little real intellect."

On August 10, Scott announced the pony assignments for the conquest of the Pole so that the handlers could get to know their animals before taking charge of them on September 1: Victor —Bowers; Snippets—Scott; Christopher—Oates; Jimmy Pigg —Keohane; Bones—Crean; Snatcher—P. O. Evans; Michael— Cherry-Garrard; Chinaman—Wright; Jehu—Atkinson; Nobby— Wilson.

Oates gave his second lecture on horse management the following day. It was brief and to the point. The horse had no reasoning power at all, he told the men, but did possess an excellent memory. Sights and sounds could evoke the circumstances under which the horse had previously seen or heard them. Memory also enabled the equines to know when they were being prepared to be used. Racehorses and hunting steeds often went off their feed and became excited before an event. It was important, therefore, to keep the ponies quiet when they were picketed during the journey. Rugs should be put on immediately on camping and removed at the last moment before the march began.

The Soldier reminded his companions that it was no use shouting at a pony. Ten to one it would associate the noise with some form of trouble and, getting excited, would set out to make more trouble. From his personal experience Oates knew it was useless to shout "whoa!" to a bucking horse. It was more important to remain firm and quiet. Even if successful, loud talk to one horse might disturb other horses.

Oates also gave the expedition hints on leading the ponies and discussed improvements for their care during the remaining weeks of the winter. A litter box, for example, might help those ponies that liked to lie down but undoubtedly found the frozen ground too cold. Before the next winter the ponies should be clipped as opposed to grooming throughout the inactive season so they would grow better coats. The Soldier then passed on to improvements in the nose bags, picketing lines, and rugs for the ponies on the forthcoming trip. He added that he intended to bandage the legs of all the ponies with putties to protect them from chafing.

Two of the most serious problems the ponies faced, however, weren't so easily solved. For snow blindness, Oates suggested dyeing

One of the nose bags used to feed the ponies

their long forelocks, but after a discussion this seemed inadequate. The best idea to emerge was to place a sunbonnet over the eyes rather than blinkers. For the obstacle of soft snow, Petty Officer Edgar Evans had been experimenting with a pair of snowshoes for Snatcher that he tried to model after his vague recollection of those worn for lawn mowing. This was a kind of stiff bag placed over the hoof. But the means of attaching this snowshoe had yet to be worked out.

In Scott's view, a slight modification of their present pony snowshoes, constructed like a racquet, would prove to be the answer. But these had one disadvantage. Made for very soft snow, they were unnecessarily large and might become strained on the Barrier's hard patches. Maybe it would be better to use the racquet type for the quiet ponies and the bag kind for the friskier ones. Petty Officer Evans (not to be confused with Lieutenant Evans)

155

experimented with the snowshoes, but they were to prove to be unworkable on the journey to the Pole. The ponies usually were too excitable to wear them. And when the men managed to get the snowshoes on a pony, the devices were damaged by the alternating soft and hard Barrier surface.

A method by which the ponies could be driven from behind instead of being led was also considered. Such a change would enable the handler to loose the connection between the pony and the sledge if the animal fell into a crevasse. But there appeared to be no way to keep the ponies pulling except by leading them, which exposed the men to great danger.

Such problems, emphasized by the loss of nine out of nineteen ponies, indicated the poor beasts were unsuitable for the task of transporting the polar party beyond the end of the ice shelf. "It was a useless risk of life" to try to take the ponies up the Beardmore Glacier, Cherry-Garrard concluded in the study of Shackleton's route that Scott requested him to make during the winter. Man-hauling the sledges appeared to be the only alternative for the most arduous phase of the quest, the 465 miles up the glacier and across the polar plateau.

By mid-August, the light at Cape Evans was beginning to increase, bolstering the spirits of the men and seemingly the animals, too. Although the sun had not yet appeared, a kind of twilight was evident for several hours around midday. In Scott's opinion, the ponies seemed so pleased to see the light while they were being exercised that they seized every opportunity to gallop off with tails and heels flung high. Even experienced hands such as Oates and Bowers couldn't manage them, and sometimes it took nearly an hour to round them up. The ponies were scheduled to be given oats, but the Soldier feared giving them any extra energy and continued the bran, which was running low.

The sun returned during a raging blizzard on August 23, and even though the men couldn't see it they toasted the event with champagne. Two days later, sun rays rested for a few minutes on the sunshine recorder for the first time since April. The men sang

U.S. NAVY

Weddell seals on the sea ice near their breathing holes

and shouted while the ponies neighed in a cacophony that must have sent Weddell seals wiggling for their breathing holes.

On the following day one of the dogs, Julick, who had been lost for a month, rushed into the station and jumped joyously over everyone. Maybe he had heard them singing. Whatever, he looked fit despite his ordeal, his mane crusted with blood and reeking of seal blubber. Had Julick been carried off on an ice floe? No one knew. What had happened to him remained an enigma. Despite this "miracle" and a few similar incidents, the Englishmen didn't change their opinion of the dogs, which they deemed losers. Meares, who had been issued runners in bad shape for his sledges, complained rather bitterly that "anything was good enough for the dogs."

10 The Quest Begins

DURING September of 1911, Scott's expedition completed about a dozen preliminary trips from Cape Evans. Most were training runs or journeys to build up supplies at Hut Point and the depots at Safety Camp and Corner Camp. A telephone line, the first in Antarctica, was laid during this period when Meares reeled off a thin aluminum wire from the back of a dog sledge he drove from Cape Evans to Hut Point. The wire held up longer than anyone expected and provided a valuable communications link between the two posts during the busy spring preparations.

Three hundred and fifty miles away, meanwhile, the Norwegians had returned to Framheim after traveling to their 80°S. depot in an unsuccessful early attempt on the Pole. They were forced back to base on September 17 because three of the men suffered frostbitten heels in spring temperatures that plunged to −68.8° F.

With the arrival of spring the ponies began shedding their coats. Nobby was the first, which Dr. Wilson, the pony's new handler, took as an indication that his pony was in the best condition. But when Wilson took Nobby out for two hours of exercise on September 29, the pony wanted to go back to the stables every few minutes and started playing pranks. Undoubtedly he felt the cold because of his new, thin coat. His favorite game was to shake his

158

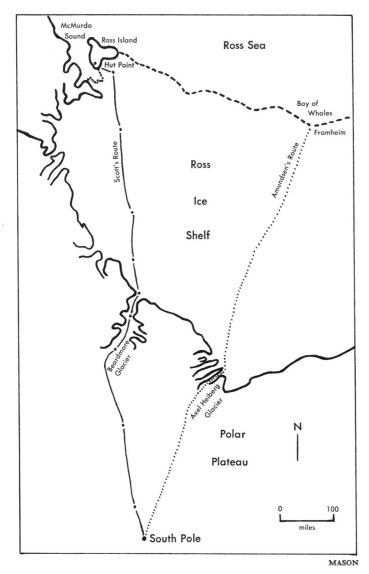

MASON

Routes of Scott's and Amundsen's parties to the Pole

head violently whenever he thought Wilson was offguard, hitting him in the face, chest, or stomach. Then the pony would try to rear and come down on Wilson's feet. The surgeon found that all he could do was hold on tightly to Nobby's head with a stiff arm to

159

stay out of reach. If Wilson tried to punch him in the ribs or threatened to hit him with the head rope, Nobby would jump toward him rather than away, and up would fly his heels. But because Wilson was positioned next to his shoulder, the pony was unable to reach him. So Nobby would then try to bite him in the leg. Wilson was perplexed by the animal's antics, for he was reputed to be one of the quietest ponies.

Oates was also having his patience strained by Christopher. On several occasions, that Manchurian monster decided he didn't want to be harnessed and galloped off. He would stop a few hundred yards from the stable and wait, watching Oates approach. As soon as the Soldier got close, Christopher would canter away. The pony eventually would tire of the game and return to the stable door. Although he had enjoyed his fun, Christopher quickly learned that Oates wasn't any pushover. The Soldier tied up a foreleg before harnessing him. To make sure he didn't tear off with the sledge, Oates kept the leg tied and made him hop on the other three for a few paces before freeing him.

Evaluating the ponies, Scott wrote ominously that he was afraid there was "much trouble in store." Although Jehu had been improving throughout the winter after having nearly died swimming ashore from the *Terra Nova*, he was still too weak to pull a loaded sledge. He looked well, but was very "weedily" built in comparison with the other ponies. Scott feared he wouldn't last long, even though a few days later Jehu easily pulled a sledge for several miles over a bad surface south of the station.

Chinaman was also pulling better than the "crock" everyone believed him to be and he was assigned to one of the smaller sledges. The others were becoming more mischievous every day due to "high living" while doing very little work except for a few preparatory sledge runs. Christopher, as would be expected, continued to become vicious, furiously biting and kicking whenever he saw a sledge. Oates eventually had to tie both forelegs and pull the pony to his knees to get him hitched.

Every day there was a "regular circus" as Oates and Anton tried

160

to break in Christopher. On one typical outing, after Oates managed to harness the pony, a dog frightened him. Christopher jerked the rope from Oates's hand and dashed away. Once free, he began twisting and turning until he dumped the two bales of fodder off the sledge. Then, with teeth bared and heels flying, he made for the other sledges, first Bowers', then Keohane's. The men ran after him to jump on the trailing sledge in an effort to slow him down. Oates, Bowers, Dr. Atkinson, and Nelson eventually succeeded in hopping on the sledge. Twisting furiously, Christopher tried to dislodge them but only managed to dump Atkinson. The other men dug their heels into the snow until they exhausted the pony. Even then, Christopher refused to give in and attacked anyone approaching his lead rope. Sometime later, Oates managed to get hold of it. Scott wrote that a little soft snow on the ice shelf would soon end such energetic capers, but he was exceedingly glad there weren't other ponies like the Manchurian monster.

Scott planned for the tractors to lead his polar party across the ice shelf, followed by the dog teams, and finally the ponies and their handlers. Day took the first tracked vehicle out to the sea ice on October 17, but the machine overran its chain and the aluminum axle casing split. So it was back to the workshop. Fortunately, the casing could be repaired. In addition to helping advance the polar party, Scott was anxious that the tractor succeed because he believed it would revolutionize polar transport. And in that he was right.

A blizzard blew in on the eighteenth, holding up Scott's departure for the Pole while he worried about Amundsen's chances of getting there first. Although he could foresee his expedition belittled by a Norwegian triumph, Scott decided to carry on as he had planned, completing as much scientific study and exploration as possible in addition to trying to win the Pole.

Scott's concern wasn't misplaced. Amundsen was preparing to depart the very next day with four companions and fifty-two dogs. Unlike Scott's forthcoming struggle across the ice shelf with the ponies, the Norwegians would be pulled over similar terrain comfortably on skis behind their dog sledges. The Englishmen also had skis but, according to Scott, they had stubbornly refused for some reason to prepare themselves to use them, although later in the journey they were forced by deep snow to do so.

Amundsen reached his first storage depot at 80°S. on October 22 while Scott still was trying to shift his party from Cape Evans to Hut Point in preparation for his final departure for the Pole. On that particular day, Nobby, Victor, and Snatcher had pulled the most important supplies to a point about halfway to Hut Point. While they were taking a break, Victor suddenly tossed his head and caught his nostril on Snatcher's harness. Then all of the ponies reared and stampeded in different directions. Snatcher galloped for Cape Evans with Petty Officer Evans in pursuit; and Nobby, leaving Dr. Wilson aghast, made for the coastal mountains across McMurdo Sound. Bowers managed to hang on as Victor dashed away in no particular direction.

Holding up a biscuit, Wilson ran after Nobby for two miles before the pony spotted the food and came trotting back to get it. Evans chased Snatcher all the way home, arriving forty minutes after the pony. But heroic little "Birdie" Bowers hung onto Victor despite the frightened animal's painful, bleeding nose and led him back to the station. When the torn flesh was cut off, the wound appeared not as serious as the blood had suggested. Victor quickly recovered and in a few days was rushing about with his sledge.

Scott as a result of this incident instructed the handlers not to leave the ponies no matter how quiet they appeared. He also ordered alterations to remove sharp points from the pony harnesses. In his diary he commented: "I don't know why our Sundays should always bring these excitements."

Next it was the tractors' turn to try to make a successful start. After more mechanical troubles, the experimental machines finally chugged up the face of the ice shelf on October 27 while the expedition cheered wildly. Scott and his party returned optimistically to Cape Evans. The first tractor, however, broke down after running only six miles south over the Barrier toward the Pole. Working all

Amundsen's party camped on the journey to the Pole. Note the wide ring of dogs.

night in a −25° F. temperature, Day and Lashly eventually got the machine operating.

By this time the Norwegians and their dogs had arrived at their 81°S. depot, putting them two hundred miles ahead in the race. Scott knew he was falling further behind Amundsen, but luck just didn't seem to be on his side. Another storm held his party at Cape Evans until October 31, when Meares left with the dogs, followed by Dr. Atkinson with Jehu and Keohane with Jimmy Pigg. This was a test to see how far Jehu could be relied on. But the former swimmer surprised everyone by easily making the transfer to Hut Point in five and a half hours.

The next morning, as Amundsen was arriving at his 82°S. depot, Scott's party finally got underway with the ponies each pulling 450 pounds. Cherry-Garrard, Dr. Wilson, and Wright departed first, leading Michael, Nobby, and Chinaman. Christopher was har-

163

HERBERT PONTING, CANTERBURY MUSEUM

Bowers and Victor

nessed with the usual difficulty and started kicking, with Oates holding on for all he was worth. It took five minutes to throw the little devil by tieing one foreleg up tight under the pony's shoulder. Then while his head was held down on the ice, the sledge was brought up behind him and Christopher was finally hitched up. Getting up on three legs, he galloped off as best he could. His bound foreleg was eventually released after several violent kicks. But once started, he couldn't be stopped. As a result, Oates, his three tent mates, and their ponies each day were forced to follow Christopher without stopping for the mid-march meal during the first 130 miles of the polar journey.

Long-legged and "very ugly," Victor also was a pain in the neck. In Bowers' words he was as nearly unmanageable as any beast could be and always likely to bolt. It took four of the men to harness Victor to a sledge and the strength of two to keep the pony from taking off once he was readied. But although Victor was skittish, he was not vicious like Christopher.

164

Bones, by contrast, ambled off gently with Crean, and Scott followed leading the still slightly lame Snippets. Petty Officer Evans with Snatcher and Bowers with Victor brought up the rear of the column that also included Anton. But as soon as Snatcher was harnessed, he began what was to become a habit of rushing ahead to take the lead. In ten minutes, Snatcher with Evans in tow passed Scott full speed. Then Bowers with Victor trotted by, leaving Scott and Snippets at the tail end.

The transit from Cape Evans to Hut Point reminded the captain of a disorganized fleet with ships of unequal speed. Scott decided to start the ponies in three groups in the future: the very slow ponies, the medium paced, and "the fliers." Snatcher arrived first at Hut Point, followed by Bones and Christopher, all finishing as fresh as they started. In fact, Oates's devil bucked and kicked all the way along the four-hour trip. Within an hour, the other ponies came in just before a blizzard struck, reaching shelter in the nick of time.

Although the veranda earlier had been extended for the ponies, Michael, Chinaman, and Jimmy Pigg were housed in the hut during the storm. Chinaman didn't appreciate this consideration and kept the men awake by stamping on the floor during the middle of the night. The tired explorers must have wished they had left him outside.

As the party departed Hut Point on the evening of November 2, a searing wind was blowing. Scott decided to march at night as the party had done during the latter stages of the depot-laying. At 8:00 P.M. Chinaman, Jehu, and Jimmy Pigg led off the historic procession on the actual start for the Pole. The slowest ponies, these three became known as the Baltic Fleet (in addition to the "crocks") due to Scott's love of maritime comparisons. Nobby, Michael, and Snippets followed two hours later. The fliers—Christopher, Victor, Snatcher, and Bones—departed last, once Christopher was subdued. Because they traveled faster, the dog teams remained behind at Hut Point for several days before starting.

The pony contingents halted individually halfway through the march for a "midnight lunch," then joined up on the ice shelf five miles beyond Safety Camp in the early morning. All the ponies, but

Scott's party camped on the Barrier

particularly Jehu and Chinaman, were tired from the trek and seemed to be off their feed, although Scott viewed this as a temporary reaction. Even though there was little wind and the sun was becoming warmer by the minute, the men built snow walls to protect the ponies. They spent several hours setting up the camp, then slept until one o'clock in the afternoon, when Scott turned them out. Serving the ponies their rations, Oates found that Bones had eaten Christopher's "goggles," leaving Christopher blinking in the hot sun. Nobby and Michael subsequently became gnawers of other ponies' fringes, too.

Scott's remaining hopes for the tractors were dashed in the early morning hours of November 4 when the party came upon the "mournful wreck" of the first abandoned machine. A note from Lieutenant Evans told the sad story: the number two cylinder had packed up and they had to push on with the one remaining vehicle, building cairns to mark the route.

The pony cavalcade pressed on, pulling heavy loads over a "cruel" soft surface most of that day. Jehu was standing up to the task better than anyone anticipated, and Chinaman was improving, too. Although subdued by the Barrier surface while underway, Christopher continued to make harnessing an ordeal that required four men to accomplish.

166

When they reached Corner Camp the following day, the ponies began to display "fanciful" appetites at feeding time. They decided the oil cake wasn't to their taste and preferred the fodder that had been cached there earlier. By the next day they no longer fancied the fodder, causing Scott to fear they would become ravenous.

To make matters worse, three black dots, which could only be the second motor machine with its two loaded sledges, had been spotted to the south. Scott was very jumpy. His fears were confirmed the next night when they reached the tracked vehicle and found its number one cylinder cracked. The engines weren't suitable for working in the antarctic climate, Scott determined, but the system of propulsion—caterpillar tracks—had proven itself. He hoped such machines would eventually abolish the use of animals in polar work, which he deemed to be cruel.

A blizzard confronted the polar party when they camped on the night of November 5. They built high, sheltering walls of snow around the ponies, and, with their new rugs, the animals seemed comfortable. Yet they continually knocked down their shelters, forcing the handlers to waste valuable rest time rebuilding.

After another stormy day, the camp was drifted with snow and the pony walls had to be dug out several times, in addition to reconstructing the sections knocked over by Snatcher and Jehu. The men discovered the walls they had built were inadequate protection from the driving snow. The fine, hard particles blew under the ponies' rugs and under their broad belly straps. Lodged in their coats, the snow melted, leaving the animals wet and miserably cold. The flying particles also tormented the ponies by bombarding their sensitive nostrils, eyes, and ears. If that wasn't enough, drifting snow covered the ponies and became ice, which was quite a chore to remove. These continual annoyances kept the ponies from resting, in Scott's belief, although in their native land such ponies have intentionally been given a coating of ice to help keep them warm.

Scott was worried about the storm's effect on the crocks, but on the next night when their rugs were stripped off, both Jehu and Chinaman appeared fresh and fit; they even enjoyed a skittish little

"Ponies on the March"

run. Chinaman also got in a playful buck before he, Jehu, and Jimmy Pigg started off with their loads at a brisk pace. The other two groups followed in due course. Surprisingly, the ponies pulled their heavy loads through the fresh soft snow with easy strides, restoring Scott's confidence in them. Most of them stopped periodically to take a mouthful of snow, particularly Michael, who was constantly at it. Then the little, highly strung Michael would rush forward in an attempt to catch up with the other ponies. Christopher, as usual, charged ahead at his "non-stop run."

Christopher had developed some new ingenious tricks to escape his harness at the start of each march. Even with all his legs tied to bring him to his knees, it still took four men several attempts to down the strong pony. He would then jump up and try to throw off the handlers, who would hang on "like grim death" despite his kicking and biting. But Christopher became more cunning each time. Finding that the soft snow didn't hurt his knees the way the sea ice had, he would plunge about at will. He would lie down at other times and wait for the men to relax their guard before jumping up and dashing away.

The trick was to get Christopher harnessed before he realized what was happening. Oates, for instance, caught him unaware at

168

FRANK DEBENHAM, SCOTT POLAR RESEARCH INSTITUTE

one point by laying the traces down the side of the sledge instead of ahead of it. The pony was harnessed and led away before he realized what had occurred. Another ruse was to hitch Christopher while he stood picketed behind the snow wall. But whatever trick was used, Christopher would invariably bolt, and hanging on proved to be a test of endurance for Oates. Christopher would seize the slightest opportunity to start kicking, even after they had traveled as far as ten miles.

During the night march of November 8, the cavalcade passed Blossom's grave, marked by a piece of black bunting on a wire. As if spooked by the ghost of the dead pony, Snatcher decided to run away as they neared their next campsite, tearing off across the slippery snow with Petty Officer Evans hanging onto the bridle. Fortunately for man and horse, there wasn't any place to run to and they soon rejoined the group. Although such exasperating incidents characterized the ponies' performance, there were some in-

FRANK DEBENHAM, SCOTT POLAR RESEARCH INSTITUTE

spiring moments, too. Bowers, for instance, added a bale of forage to Victor's sledge from the other loads, bringing the weight to nearly eight hundred pounds. Victor stepped out again as though he didn't notice the additional burden.

As the march continued, Scott noted the absence of places where the ponies sank to their hocks in the snow, which Shackleton had described in his experience of trekking across the Barrier. The snow surface so far had been very good by comparison, and the ponies rarely sank to the fetlock joint. For this reason, Scott tended to discount Shackleton's reports, although he realized that another inch of snow would make a tremendous difference.

The crocks surprised everyone when they played up during the next night's march. Wright left Chinaman momentarily to examine the distance indicated on his sledgemeter. The pony evidently didn't like being left behind the other ponies and stampeded toward them with Wright running after him. Seeing that he was the only one remaining, Jehu decided to follow. The astounded men watched the old pony they believed to be on his last legs set off "at a sprawling canter in Chinaman's wake."

11 Poor Beasts

ONLY a few days after commenting on Shackleton's trouble with the frozen surface of the ice shelf, Scott began to experience it himself: "A worse set of conditions for the ponies could scarcely be imagined." In addition to soft, newly fallen snow, patches of soft crust were interspersed with areas of ice-hard sastrugi. Snow lay like "sandy heaps" in pits between these places. Due to an overcast sky, the light was also bad, compounding the difficulty. The pony groups at times followed in each other's tracks and saw one another only at camp. Despite these conditions, the strong ponies pulled well and the crocks managed nine and a half miles on the march. The dogs were running splendidly, covering twenty miles during the night from one camp to the next.

The column on the night of November 11 passed the cairn where Blucher had been buried on the way to Bluff Depot eight months earlier. A mile beyond the depot, Dr. Atkinson and Wright halted with the crocks. Chinaman in their estimation wouldn't last another mile or two. But the pony managed three miles to the camp for the night, where Oates had a look at him and predicted he had many days left. On hearing the report, Scott accepted it, but he was more pessimistic himself. "They are not the ponies they ought to have been," he lamented.

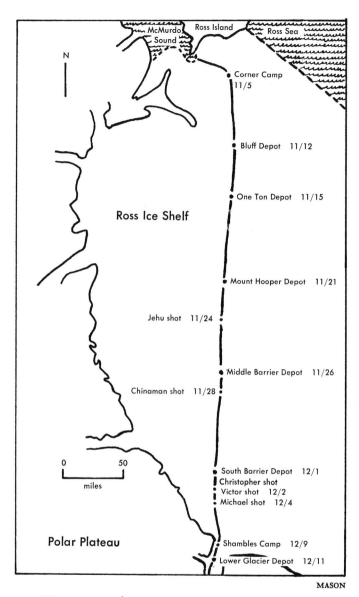

N

McMurdo Sound
Ross Island
Ross Sea

• Corner Camp
11/5

• Bluff Depot   11/12

• One Ton Depot   11/15

Ross Ice Shelf

• Mount Hooper Depot   11/21

Jehu shot   11/24 •

• Middle Barrier Depot   11/26

Chinaman shot   11/28 •

0   50
miles

• South Barrier Depot   12/1
Christopher shot
Victor shot   12/2
Michael shot   12/4

Polar Plateau

• Shambles Camp   12/9
• Lower Glacier Depot   12/11

The Scott party's outward march across the Barrier

Pressing on, the men tried to remain cheerful as falling snow added more inches to the troublesome surface. The ponies gallantly plunged ahead, but it was a painful effort. The only bright note

172

during these night marches was that Oates had fooled Christopher into being harnessed three times without difficulty, a record feat in the deadly game between Oates and the Manchurian monster.

The strain quickly began to tell on the horses. When they were examined on November 13, the handlers found all were wearing out. Victor had become lean and lanky, and "ancient" Chinaman looked as though he should have been on a pension. Although Jehu appeared rocky, he had gone farther than anyone imagined and so had earned the nickname of the "Barrier Wonder." To Oates the ponies were "the most unsuitable scrap-heap crowd of unfit creatures that could possibly be got together."

On the morning of the fifteenth, the party reached One Ton Depot, 150 miles from Cape Evans. It was painfully obvious that Chinaman and the Barrier Wonder wouldn't make it much farther. In addition, the dogs were running short of food and the ponies would have to be killed to keep them alive. When Scott made the decision to take only enough pony food to get the ponies to the Beardmore Glacier, his companions were much relieved. The men had feared it would be suicidal to lead ponies up the lower reaches of the Beardmore, which Shackleton had reported were so heavily crevassed. No one doubted Shackleton's judgment in this respect.

The ponies won a well-deserved day's rest at One Ton Depot, and a hundred pounds of fodder were left behind to lighten their loads. The loads were also rearranged so that the stronger ponies carried 580 pounds while the others pulled about 400. Although their condition had ebbed more quickly than he anticipated, Oates believed the ponies could make it to the Beardmore. Scott was equally confident. In fact, he thought most of the ponies were actually in better form than when they started. Only the crocks were cause for alarm.

After One Ton Depot, for a few days the surface was better for the ponies, partially due to rising summer temperatures (up to 20° F.) that tended to melt any fresh snow on the crust. The warm sun also dried the equipment on the sledges, improving the men's comfort. Wearing goggles for protection from the glare, the party was further cheered by a clear view of the mountains marking the southern boundary of the ice shelf. In the bright sunshine everything at least looked more hopeful. If the men had known that Amundsen's party already had reached these distant mountains, their cheer would have been diminished.

During the next three days, while the Norwegians and their dogs were climbing the Axel Heiberg Glacier to the polar plateau, Scott's expedition began struggling through very deep snow further northeast. Often the ponies sank halfway to their hocks, and Jehu stopped every few hundred yards. Big icicles formed on the ponies' noses during the march. To help Chinaman, Wright took off his windproof blouse and turned it into a handkerchief that he tied around the pony's nose. Forcing the ponies on was "a funeral business," requiring patience and care. Scott feared the horses were carrying too much food, so when the men struck camp on November 18, a sack of feed (probably weighing one hundred pounds) was cached there, against Bowers' judgment.

The Barrier Wonder was nearly done in by the time the party stopped on the nineteenth. Michael, the littlest pony, also had been floundering badly. Twice he sank nearly up to his hocks in snow. Victor was looking very gaunt, although Nobby appeared stronger than ever. Nobby downed his feed and as much more as he could get from the other ponies or the handlers. Dr. Wilson took pity on him and during the following days gave him an extra box of biscuits. In Cherry-Garrard's opinion, Nobby had an easier time because he had gained earlier experience of the ice shelf conditions during the depot-laying the previous summer. Christopher, on the other hand, was too obstinate to let the surface bother him very much. Demonstrating his healthy condition, he kicked in the bow of the sledge as he neared the end of the march on November 20.

A better surface on the following night brought an improvement in the ponies' state, making it "impossible not to take a hopeful view of their prospect of pulling through," wrote Scott. But he was not as fortunate with the remaining tractor. Three miles beyond Mount Hooper Depot, established earlier by the motor party, Scott found Lieutenant Evans and his emaciated men who had been waiting six days for Scott's group to catch up. After the last tracked vehicle broke down, they had man-hauled their sledges. It was evident from the appearance of Day and Hooper that the food ration allotted for all of the men was insufficient for those doing the hard work of pulling sledges. But Scott wasn't overly concerned because he planned to increase the ration once the party started up the Beardmore.

Lieutenant Evans and his two companions joined the pony handlers and started ahead of the ponies to make a track with their sledges, even though Scott planned to send Day and Hooper back in a few days. He expected the Barrier Wonder to cave in about the same time, leaving the party with an extra sledge. Meares, who had been anticipating the event, looked forward to feeding his dogs a good meal. But Dr. Atkinson and Oates were equally keen to get Jehu beyond the point where Shackleton had been forced to kill his first pony. Since Chinaman had perked up, they had hopes for that persistent pony, whom the men jokingly called the "Thunderbolt." The Englishmen obviously hadn't lost their particular sense of humor despite their ordeal.

Amundsen's party had climbed 10,920 feet to the top of the Axel Heiberg Glacier by this time and was approaching the polar plateau. Believing they had already reached the plateau, Amundsen ordered twenty-four of his forty-two dogs killed as planned. Fourteen of the carcasses were depoted at what they called Butcher's Shop and the rest fed to the surviving dogs. Although Amundsen is generally depicted as ruthless, he reacted as sensitively as Scott did to such "necessary killings." He pumped up the primus stove in an attempt to drown out the shots while he prepared supper in the tent: "There went the first shot—I am not a nervous man, but I must admit that I gave a start." His men were sad and depressed that evening, when they should have been rejoicing at their accomplishment of reaching what they thought to be the polar plateau. (They had another tough two weeks of traversing before making the actual plateau.) And it was the next day before they

Underway across the ice shelf. Christopher, unidentified, is one of these ponies.

could force themselves to eat the dog cutlets.

Scott, at this stage 150 miles from the beginning of his glacier route, began to weigh the pros and cons of night marching. The ponies benefited from resting during the warmest part of the day in temperatures a few degrees above zero. Yet they had to work harder to pull the sledges at night because of increased friction on the runners when the surface particles began to freeze into a soft crust, particularly in the hours before and after midnight. "Night-time" temperatures dropped to $-14°$ F. as the sun circled to a low position on the horizon. The soft crust was also a problem because it wouldn't give way until the full weight of a pony was on it. Then the pony would sink an average of eight inches into the snow. The animals fortunately were becoming more accustomed to the new crust and plodded on, showing less irritation than at first.

All of the little horses had lost weight and their rotundity, despite their fill of oats and oil cake. They were fed by their handlers at the lunch and supper halts, then by Oates and Bowers when the company camped to sleep. Some of them developed the annoying habit of tossing off their nose bags, either because they didn't want to wear them to begin with or because they were trying to reach the maize left at the bottom. To stop them, the men had to tie the feed bags onto their bridles.

Victor joined the ranks of head-rope chewers, although Bowers maintained he couldn't be hungry because he wouldn't eat all of his

176

ration. The once-spirited pony had become a "steady goer" and as gentle as a "dear old sheep" after three weeks on the Barrier. Like Christopher, he had been tamed by the struggle across the featureless ice shelf. Victor now led the pony column, just as Bowers' former pony, Uncle Bill, had done during the depot-laying. Bowers, who could hardly believe the change in Victor, became more fond of the pony than ever and wouldn't have traded him for any other.

The weather was gloriously sunny as the group traveled on, prompting Scott to start off later each night with the idea of eventually changing over to daytime marching. Although they sank "cruelly" into the snow at times, the ponies were going steadily and the men were being careful not to overwork them. But Jehu, the "crockiest of the crocks," was pulling very little. When the party camped on the evening of November 24, Scott decided the most merciful thing to do was to put him out of his misery. The Barrier Wonder had reached fifteen miles beyond the point where Shackleton had been forced to shoot his first pony on November 21, 1908. Despite the ability to continue on a little farther, Jehu was led back on the track and shot.

After being a doubtful starter, Jehu had turned in a surprising performance, which Cherry-Garrard credited to the pony's "good spirit." His ability to have "dragged his poor body so far" also was due to a triumph of management by Oates and Dr. Atkinson. Bowers added that Jehu hadn't been treated cruelly. The Barrier Wonder had been given a year's care and fed well. Only three weeks of work had been demanded of him, and except for his swim ashore from the *Terra Nova* he had been well cared for before his "painless end."

Dr. Atkinson, since his pony was gone, joined Lieutenant Evans and Lashly in man-hauling their gear on a ten-foot sledge. Day and Hooper were sent back to Hut Point with two weakening dogs and a note from Scott saying he was taking the dog teams on further than he originally intended because of the additional food in the form of horse meat. Jehu had provided four meals for the dogs; another such supply would sustain the huskies all the way to the

Beardmore. The Barrier Wonder had come up "trumps after all," and this sealed Chinaman's fate.

The next day, November 26, Middle Barrier Depot was established, 290 miles from Cape Evans, and the expedition plunged on through worsening surface conditions and deteriorating weather. The men tried their skis, which became hopelessly clogged. The ponies sank several inches through the soft snow to the hard surface underneath. But the dogs had no trouble at all. They started the march last and whizzed along. Watching them coming into camp at night after the ponies had been tethered and fed, Oates would murmur that he would give the huskies another ten days before they, too, played out.

Chinaman finally made his exit on November 28, less than ninety miles from the Beardmore. Wright, who had led the pony, maintained that the Thunderbolt never shirked his duty and was quite capable of reaching the glacier. Nonetheless, the old pony was shot and provided four meals for the twenty remaining dogs. Some of the tenderloin was saved to be used later in the men's hoosh. Wright joined the man-hauling group as its navigator, despite snow blindness in his right eye. Chinaman's ten-foot sledge was taken on by little Michael, whose twelve-foot sledge was placed over some remains left for the return trip.

Victor and Christopher by this time had become the weakest ponies. Christopher, it seems, had run out of energy. Bones and Nobby were deemed the strongest. Nobby and Snippets began walking by themselves in the tracks of the column without being led. They carefully watched their handlers and stopped the moment they did, and it was a big relief not to have to lead them.

Some days were utterly miserable, such as one described by Bowers when Victor started "as slow as a funeral horse." The light was so intense that Bowers had to wear goggles, which the driving snow filled up as fast as he could clear them. His fear that Victor would give out was like a nightmare as they dropped a long way behind the others. After four excruciating miles of these conditions, he was fed up but said little at the halt because everybody else was also disgusted. But following the break, Victor stepped out at a "good swinging pace" despite the surface and led the line in his customary place. He went equally well in the afternoon. When they camped and his harness was removed, Victor enjoyed a roll in the snow, something he hadn't done in ten or twelve days. "It certainly does not look like exhaustion!" Bowers observed.

Nearing the Beardmore, the ponies began sinking up to their knees in the snow and were tiring rapidly. They also were outlasting their forage. So Scott, against some opposition, decided Christopher had to go. Some of the men apparently believed Christopher could be taken further, although they regretted his departure less than that of the other ponies. In addition to the trouble he had caused, the Manchurian monster never pulled his share of the load across the Barrier.

The expedition left the extra sledge and a week's food cached with Christopher's bones at what they named Southern Barrier Depot on December 1, thereby reducing the weight that the surviving ponies had to pull. When they departed the following morning, snowshoes were tried on Nobby, who did about four miles in them before the "wretched affairs racked" and had to be taken off. Scott still believed the ponies would have been in good shape if they had been able to wear some sort of snowshoes from the beginning.

As they continued on, the ponies seemed to be encouraged by the view of the spectacular western mountains, sparkling in the bright sunshine. Many cliffs with yellow-brown or dark-brown rocks were exposed, which tended to break up the monotony of the barren white landscape. Among the enormous glaciers cutting deeply through the snow-covered range, the expedition could see the mighty Beardmore, flowing into the ice shelf that it helped to form. But for the ponies this sight meant the end of the line.

Before breaking camp on December 2, Scott told Bowers that he had come to a decision which would shock him. Victor had to go next because of the feed shortage. "It seemed an awful pity to have to shoot a great strong animal," Bowers wrote of his pony. He hoped he would do as well as Victor had done when he replaced the

179

animal in the harness. His Victor always had had a biscuit, and Bowers gave him a final one before he was led away.

The meat provided five meals for the dogs and a nourishing hoosh for the men on the following day. Although it had taken them awhile, all of the men now were willing to eat the horse meat and, in Scott's words, were "so well fed" that hunger wasn't thought of, but only for the moment.

Although hunger had been subdued temporarily, the weather remained indomitable. Blizzards stymied the expedition on December 3. But despite the accumulation of new snow, after the storms the surviving six ponies marched thirteen miles without difficulty, causing Scott to believe they were in better shape than Shackleton's ponies had been. He didn't doubt the ponies could go on for many miles if food allowed, yet it was his decision to leave behind a sack of feed at One Ton Depot to lighten the sledges. When the huskies arrived ravenous in camp on the fourth, however, he felt Michael had to be sacrificed. The men, their bodies exhausted by the tough trek and cold, were also looking forward to more proper food after weeks of existing on dried rations.

"Gallant little Michael," as Cherry-Garrard called his worn-out charge, had been a good friend. He also had a good record of performance, although to the last moment he was chewing up everything he could reach. The young zoologist believed life had been a constant wonder to Michael and no movement in camp ever escaped his notice.

The men crawled into their sleeping bags wishing for one clear day to traverse the remaining twelve miles to the gap in the mountains that Shackleton had called the Gateway. One good march and the ponies' agony would be over. But when they woke in the morning of December 5, the men found fortune's wheel had turned against them once more. A blizzard screaming down on them trapped them for four miserable days at what Scott called Desolation Camp. If they stepped out of their tents for a couple of minutes, they were completely covered with sticky, sleet-like snow, due to temperatures that rose to 31° F. In most regions of the world

Cherry-Garrard and Michael

warm weather would have been welcomed enthusiastically; here it was disastrous. The ponies soon were soaked and, when the temperature dropped slightly, their exposed heads, tails, and legs were covered with ice. To give them some relief, the men grappled in the blinding snow to rebuild the shelter wall; Scott was determined to minimize their suffering until the end.

With all their gear wet, the men were "miserable, utterly miserable," in Scott's description. Keohane composed a rhyme in an attempt to make light of their grim predicament:

> The snow is all melting and everything's afloat,
> If this goes on much longer we shall have to turn
>   the *tent* upside down and use it as a boat.

As the temperature rose to 33° F., the wet snow continued to

181

accumulate, climbing higher on the ponies' backs and on their shelter. Only one small meal remained for the animals after they were fed on the third day of the tempest. The party either had to march on the next day or sacrifice their charges. The men already had begun to consume their precious rations allotted for the trek up the Beardmore—rations that were calculated to the ounce and irreplaceable. "Resignation to misfortune is the only attitude, but not an easy one to adopt," Scott wrote. Even if he could replan the journey, however, he claimed that he wouldn't have changed anything. All previous experience indicated December would be their "finest month."

A break in the weather finally came the next afternoon, December 8, and the men struggled through drifts often waist deep to find the sledges and dig them out. Four of those who had been man-hauling tried to pull one load but sank up to their knees in the snow. When they tried to harness Nobby to a sledge, he floundered up to his belly, and that idea was squelched. Despite what they had been through, the ponies appeared "wonderfully fit" and looked around "wistfully" for more to eat. Their ration had been cut in half to last one more day in hopes the weather would improve enough to enable them to make the Beardmore. Although he knew that his Nobby was to be shot after one more march, while he himself had to go on for days, Dr. Wilson fed him all five of his own biscuits that night.

The party finally got underway at eight o'clock in the morning, with the men forced to use their skis. The ponies were stiff from standing through the blizzard and hungry from being fed on half their usual allotment. Their feed that morning was lamented by Wilson as "a mere apology for a ration." In such condition, the ponies faced the worst day of the journey. The men tried to coax the animals into leading the way because of the danger of crevasses. But none would plunge ahead for more than a few minutes at a time. Following their handlers, however, they did fairly well.

For the first mile the man-haulers painfully tried to take the lead through the soft snow; then Petty Officer Evans rescued the wal-

Captain Oates and Snippets, one of the ponies that survived until Shambles Camp

lowing column by putting the last pair of snowshoes on Snatcher. After a little admonishing, the valiant pony led the way with the others following in his wake, a few hundred yards at a time. Nevertheless, Snippets slipped as far as his hindquarters into a chasm, but he was quickly unharnessed and pulled to safety.

According to Dr. Wilson, it was horrible work flogging the ponies on. Floundering belly deep, the tired animals constantly collapsed, lay down, or sank in the snow. The party pressed on all day without taking the risk of halting for lunch. At one point, the men couldn't get the ponies to move more than five or six yards without stopping. Scott finally called an end to the ordeal at eight o'clock in the evening, when they were within a mile of the slope ascending to the gap in the mountains. At this place they made Shambles Camp, so named because they were forced to shoot the exhausted ponies due to lack of forage. Praising them in his diary,

183

Scott said, "Poor beasts! They have done wonderfully well considering the terrible circumstances under which they worked, but yet it is hard to have to kill them so early."

Scott's pony Snippets, whose blubber-eating topped the list of the strange items devoured by the ponies, was one of these last five ponies to be shot. Jimmy Pigg and Nobby, the veterans who had survived the depot-laying journey across the ice shelf, were also destroyed, as were Bones and Snatcher.

Once the grisly job had been done, Dr. Wilson congratulated Oates for his outstanding work in caring for the ponies throughout the expedition. "And *I* thank you," Scott added as they stood under the shadow of Mount Hope. The Soldier grunted and was pleased.

The men were determinedly optimistic, but, ahead of them, Amundsen and his dog teams were already on the polar plateau, past Shackleton's furthest point south, and had laid their final depot at 88°25′ S.

12 Winners and Losers

BOLSTERED by the pony meat, Scott's dogs were traveling so well that the English leader planned to take them part of the way up the Beardmore. But gaining the lower part of the glacier on December 10, the party encountered a distressing amount of soft snow. The men sank up to their knees and the sledges went in as far as the bow. Here Shackleton had found hard blue ice. "It seems an extraordinary difference in fortune, and at every step S.'s luck becomes more evident," Scott noted. So the dog teams, although fit, were ordered back to Cape Evans the next day after Lower Glacier Depot had been set up. With them Scott sent a note saying the expedition's fortune must change and that he was keeping up with the others, who were younger. For some time he had worried about his capacity to endure the climb to the Pole. Scott was forty-three. But reassuringly he kept in mind that Peary was fifty-two when he finally conquered the North Pole.

The men now became the ponies as they harnessed themselves to the three remaining sledges and strapped on their skis, which kept them from becoming hopelessly bogged down. Nearly jerking their insides out, they pulled the sledges up the awesome glacier. On December 21, they established Upper Glacier Depot at eight thou-

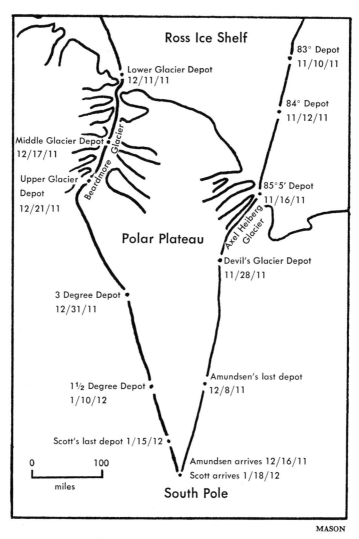

Ross Ice Shelf

83° Depot
11/10/11

Lower Glacier Depot
12/11/11

84° Depot
11/12/11

Middle Glacier Depot
12/17/11

Beardmore Glacier

Upper Glacier
Depot
12/21/11

85°5' Depot
11/16/11

Polar Plateau

Axel Heiberg Glacier

Devil's Glacier Depot
11/28/11

3 Degree Depot
12/31/11

Amundsen's last depot
12/8/11

1½ Degree Depot
1/10/12

Scott's last depot 1/15/12

0   100
miles

Amundsen arrives 12/16/11
Scott arrives 1/18/12

South Pole

Routes of Scott's and Amundsen's parties through the Transantarctic Mountains to the South Pole

sand feet above sea level, and Scott picked Dr. Atkinson, Wright, Keohane, and Cherry-Garrard to return to Cape Evans because of the limited food rations. All were terribly disappointed, even though they knew only a few could go on. They had endured so much and had come so close without the reward of reaching the Pole.

Scott and seven companions pushed on. Christmas they celebrated with a four-course meal that included horse-meat stew
flavored with onion and curry powder and thickened with biscuit.
After what was a big meal for them, they found it difficult to return
to pulling sledges that weighed 750 pounds.

At an altitude of 10,180 feet on January 3, 1912, the men were
about 165 miles from their prize. But on the next day Scott was
forced by the food situation to send back Lieutenant Evans and
Lashly, as well as Crean who wept openly. It was particularly tough
on Evans and Lashly; they had man-hauled a loaded sledge all the
way from near Corner Camp, about 680 miles. Scott originally had
planned to make the final assault with three companions, but at the
last minute he chose four. The additional choice is believed to have
been Oates, even though the Soldier was not the most fit because of
an old war wound that had flared up, causing him to limp. Some
historians have suggested Oates was included as a reward for his
hard work with the ponies that had enabled the expedition to reach
within striking distance of the Pole.

Before Lieutenant Evans' group departed, Oates gave instructions to Lashly on the care and management of the mules that were
to arrive on the relief ship. Scott, with Petty Officer Evans, Dr.
Wilson, and Oates, continued on skis, with Bowers hustling to keep
up on foot. Bowers' skis had been depoted on December 30 to

*Scott, Evans, Oates, and Wilson man-hauling their sledge, taken by
Bowers*

SCOTT POLAR RESEARCH INSTITUTE

Scott and his men find a tent flying the Norwegian flag upon their arrival at the South Pole.

lighten the sledges. The incredible Marine had to work even harder than the others because of his short legs. He certainly had realized his hope, made when Victor was shot, that he would do as well as his pony when the time came for him to pull the sledge.

Scott's party neared the South Pole on January 16, after enduring hunger, exhaustion, frostbite, and blistering cold. Few journeys in history have been so arduous. Achievement seemed assured.

188

Then the sharp-eyed Bowers spotted a black speck in the distance. Rushing toward it, they found a well-frayed black flag on a tent marking the remains of a camp. There were tracks of skis and dogs all around it. The Norwegians obviously had made it first. "It is a terrible disappointment, and I am very sorry for my loyal companions," Scott wrote.

They had two days' march to the Pole's actual location, where they found another Norwegian tent and a note from Amundsen asking Scott to forward an attached letter to the King of Norway as proof of the Norwegian victory! Being a gentleman, Scott accepted the duty, even though he considered Amundsen a usurper. "Great God! this is an awful place and terrible enough for us to have laboured to it without the reward of priority. Well, it is something to have got here. . . ." Scott, too, left a note in the tent, took pictures, and, after checking the Norwegians' positioning of the Pole started the grueling trip back to Cape Evans. Because of weight limitations only enough food had been cached at each depot along the route to take them on to the next supply. Any major delays would be fatal. "I wonder if we can do it," the defeated leader confessed.

Amundsen and his companions' conquest of the Pole hadn't been a picnic, but they had suffered far less hardship than the English expedition. They had some timely luck on their side, too, particularly in choosing the unexplored Axel Heiberg Glacier route through the mountains, which turned out to be much easier going than the Shackleton-Scott track. By the time Scott's party arrived at the Pole, the Norwegians were virtually sailing across the ice shelf toward Framheim, where they arrived on January 25. They had so much food for both men and dogs that masses of biscuits were "thrown about." Seal meat was also plentiful and the dogs were given extra food, including chocolate, a small reward in turn for the great triumph they had gained for their masters.

The victors had packed up and sailed from the Bay of Whales for Australia while Scott and his band were battling their way back across the polar plateau toward the summit of the hateful Beard-

Defeated by the Norwegians, Scott's men pose at the South Pole for a photograph taken by pulling a string. Sitting (left to right) *are Bowers and Wilson; standing are Evans, Scott, and Oates.*

more. Although they could travel more quickly down the glacier, the Englishmen found the descent more difficult and dangerous than the way up. Midway down the river of ice they began falling into crevasses nearly every minute, causing delays that further eroded their dwindling food supply. Despite careful planning, Scott, as with Shackleton, hadn't taken enough food to cover setbacks in their schedule. Still, Scott's party took the time to collect thirty-five pounds of important geological specimens, containing fossilized leaves, from the mountains bordering the Beardmore.

Edgar Evans, who sustained a concussion and had frostbitten hands, collapsed and died on February 17. The only enlisted man among the polar party, the others viewed him as the strong man of

190

the expedition, although Bowers seems to be more deserving of that title. Some hours later, the four survivors made it to Lower Glacier Depot, got some sleep, and continued on to Shambles Camp, where the last ponies had been killed. Here there was horse flesh to sustain them and a better sledge to help them travel. That night they fixed a stew of pemmican and horse meat which they voted the best hoosh eaten on the journey. But they were still three hundred miles from their main supply camp, One Ton Depot. If they weren't delayed further by injuries or the weather, Cherry-Garrard and Demetri would be waiting there with the dogs, but not for long because of Scott's strict orders that the dogs were not to be risked. Even though he considered them unreliable, Scott needed the huskies to support the mules during the following summer's work.

Scott's party trudged on toward South Barrier Depot in a race against starvation and the Antarctic winter which was about to unfetter its fury. Scott wrote that it was great luck having a bit of horse meat to add to their pitiable ration, even though they were short on fuel needed to cook it. In temperatures plummeting to −40° F. the men continued the trek, cheered only by the "splendid pony hoosh" at bedtime. But there was little meat left at this point. Nearly all of it had been used to feed the dogs or taken with the men on the journey toward the Pole. Had some been cached on the Barrier, hunger wouldn't have been a problem for the returning polar party.

Reaching Middle Barrier Depot on March 1, the Englishmen found a considerable loss of oil from the cans stored there, which forced them to work in low temperatures without a hot meal. Had the fuel leaked? Or had the returning support parties used too much? Although the situation was becoming critical, Scott didn't blame anyone. Then Oates revealed that he had badly frostbitten toes. For days he had been marching silently in pain; now, instead of pulling, he had to walk beside the sledge, resting when the others searched frozen tracks in the snow to determine their direction. Although they all continued to put on the mask of hopefulness, their chances for surviving were rapidly deteriorating.

CAVALRY AND GUARDS CLUB. BY PERMISSION

*Dollman's painting of Oates's sacrifice, "A Very Gallant Gentleman,"
hangs in the Cavalry and Guards Club, London.*

On March 9, the four men arrived at Mount Hooper Depot to find shortages in all the cached rations. Whatever the cause, it was another blow to their hopes of reaching One Ton Depot, now seventy-two miles away. As they forged on, their physical condition was running down and the cold was intensifying. The bitter March wind pierced their patched garments. Oates had become a hinderance, but the others gallantly urged him to keep going, even though Scott ordered Dr. Wilson to issue the means for each man to end his agony if the time came. Scott and Oates chose thirty opium tablets apiece, whereas Bowers and Wilson each selected a tube of morphine.

The following day, as they grappled on, Cherry-Garrard and Demetri left One Ton Depot with the dogs after waiting there a week and returned to Hut Point. Cherry-Garrard had no other choice. He, Demetri, and the dogs were in bad shape and short of food; they couldn't touch the supplies left for the returning polar party. Later, he never forgave himself because he did not disobey Scott and, killing the dogs for food along the way, strike "blindly

192

south" in hopes of finding the dying men.

Oates, meantime, was plodding on the best he could with his companions. He begged them to leave him at an old pony camp on March 15, but they forced him to go on another few miles. The next morning, when they woke during a blizzard, Oates announced he was going outside the tent and might be "some time." He was never seen again. Having previously discussed what should be done in such a situation, the men knew he had sacrificed himself for them.

After a final supreme effort, the remaining three men pushed to within eleven miles of One Ton Depot on March 21 before a blizzard trapped them, swirling drifts of snow around their tent continuously for eight days. Their meager food and fuel lasted only a few days. Severely weakened, Scott made his last diary entry on March 29. They had decided to "stick it out to the end" and die naturally, after Dr. Wilson objected to the drugs. "The end cannot be far. . . . For God's sake look after our people."

13 The Search

AFTER Cherry-Garrard and Demetri returned in poor shape from replenishing One Ten Depot, one more rescue mission was undertaken to look for the polar party. Dr. Atkinson, now in command, and Keohane added a week's provisions eight miles south of Corner Camp on March 30, one day after Scott's last diary entry. Convinced Scott and his companions had perished, they returned to base. The winter was closing in, making it impossible to continue looking.

The *Terra Nova*, meanwhile, had arrived on February 9 with eleven dogs and seven Himalayan mules that Scott had ordered. Intended for a third season of exploration, the mules now became crucial in the search for the missing men. When the ship sailed on March 4, many of the thirteen men who remained to face another winter believed the mules were their only hope of finding Scott's group in the spring. They thought the polar party probably had perished on the Beardmore Glacier, making it necessary for the rescue party to haul supplies across the ice shelf. And for this they needed the mules.

Although the mules had been carefully prepared in India, they proved to be high-spirited and excitable, especially during the win-

The Indian Army mules on Quail Island before the voyage to Antarctica

ter when they were taken out for exercise. But these animals were always anxious to get outside, which would have been insanity to the ponies. The mules were also given to fits of jealousy whenever they thought another animal was getting more attention. Pyaree was the worst. When she was kept indoors because of a "housemaid's knee," she took revenge on her companions by biting each hard while on the way out of the stables and again on returning.

Gulab was skittish whereas others such as Lal Khan were playful; their favorite game was running around their handlers, then stopping to paw the ground as if teasing the men. Khan Sahib was forever yawning, as though suffering from "polar ennui"! But all of the mules enjoyed two good friends: Lashly, who groomed and fed them every day, and the dog Vaida, who would go through the stables rubbing noses with each mule in the line.

When the sun returned to Cape Evans, Dr. Atkinson sent supplies and mule fodder with the dog teams to Corner Camp. Then the mules were transferred to Hut Point and on October 29, 1912, the search party began night-marching as Scott had done. Wright,

195

Eye shades used to help protect the mules against snow blindness, found on Ross Island along with hobbles and a waddy, or crop, presumably used to wack the animals

who was an able navigator as well as a physicist, commanded the mule column, with Abdullah leading.

At Corner Camp, additional stores were loaded so that each mule was dragging a three months' supply of provisions, nearly seven hundred pounds each. Although the party had new sledges with tapered runners that appeared to make pulling easier, the

Mule party readies to search for Scott and his companions.

196

weather was colder than during the preceding year and the bright sun inflicted snow blindness. The mules' eating habits were affected, too. They refused to touch their oil cake and oats and, reminiscent of the ponies, developed goat-like appetites for such items as their rugs, tea leaves, and men's clothing. Rani and Abdullah were great rope-eaters, dividing a rope between them during the halts. Lal Khan had a gourmet's taste for nothing but sugar. The mules were also as clever as the ponies. They soon learned to pull their picketing buckles apart and then would wander about the camp as they pleased.

The rescue party arrived at One Ton Depot on November 11, after traveling two weeks, nearly the same time it had taken Scott and the ponies. On the next morning, Wright used his binoculars to observe a curious-looking cairn with bamboo poles sticking up eleven miles south of the depot. This, as he feared, turned out to be the tent of the polar party.

When the rescuers reached the site, Dr. Atkinson took Scott's diaries and read the tragic fate of their countrymen. They covered the bodies with the outer tent, read a burial service, and built a large snow cairn with a cross of skis above it. After a record was placed in a metal cylinder, the rescue party searched twenty miles south for Oates's body. They found the Soldier's sleeping bag on one of the old pony walls, recognizable as merely a ridge in the surface of the snow. But since the sleeping bag had been carried on by the others after Oates walked out into the blizzard, the rescue party continued thirteen miles on to the camp where he had sacrificed

himself. There, they found snow had covered everything. So they built a cairn to the memory of the ponies' manager and on it placed a small cross and a record of his death.

The rescue party sadly turned back to Cape Evans. At times the mules sank deep into the snow, slowing the return march. But more seriously, they wouldn't eat properly while on the Barrier. The explorers tried just about everything, including feeding them dog biscuits. As long as the mules thought the men weren't looking they gobbled the biscuits, but as soon as the obstinate animals realized they were meant to eat the biscuits, they would go on their hunger strike again.

Lal Khan, who refused to eat anything, and Khan Sahib, who couldn't keep up with the others, were shot near Bluff Depot. The remaining five were destroyed on January 19, 1913, when the *Terra Nova* returned for the last time to bring the survivors of this epic home. Although their performance indicated the mules would have been no more successful than the ponies for Antarctic work, they had played a vital historical role. Without them, the world might not have known what became of Scott and his companions.

Before he died, Scott had written that the causes of the disaster weren't due to faulty organization but to misfortune. He blamed, first of all, the loss of the ponies during the depot-laying, which forced him to start late on the journey to the Pole because he couldn't afford risking the surviving ponies in the early-season temperatures. The reduced pony transport subsequently limited the provisions that the men were able to take with them. They also had bad luck with the weather and the accumulation of soft snow at various stages, making it a grueling trip for both men and beasts.

As Amundsen had demonstrated with his dog teams, the ponies were a poorer choice for transportation over the antarctic terrain. Although they came from a harsh northern environment, the ponies had trouble adapting to the more hostile Antarctic with its alternating soft and hard surfaces, crevasses, monotonous landscape, and lack of forage under the snow. The animals were in questionable condition to begin with. They were too old and had had a life of abuse and neglect. Then they were shipped a great distance, arriving in Antarctica weak and knocked about. They also had thin coats, which may have been caused by the reversal of the seasons between the Northern and Southern Hemispheres. Too much was expected of them.

Not enough time was allowed for the ponies to be properly broken in or trained to pull sledges while the expedition was in New Zealand. Few of the men had much knowledge of horses or ponies; none of them knew anything about the Manchurian breed. And both Shackleton and Scott had known from others' experiences that the ponies would be troublesome. But the English leaders were prejudiced by the advantage of the animals' potential hauling power and relied on them instead of dog teams, the usual mode of polar transport. As a result, the ponies caused delays that prevented both explorers from obtaining their goal. In the case of Scott, the delays cost him his life and that of his four companions. His polar party most likely would have survived if One Ton Depot had been situated farther south or if he had been able to start earlier on the journey with a large number of dogs to carry them swiftly across the Barrier. Huskies, because they weighed less than the ponies, would have had less trouble from sinking into the snow and would have required less care.

Equines of any kind were never again used in the Antarctic, although dog teams continue to serve in a limited capacity. Only the evidence of the presence of the Manchurian ponies remains in the McMurdo Sound area, evoking the heroic struggle for the conquest of the South Pole. In the vicinity of Shackleton's hut at Cape Royds, some bales of fodder, boxes of maize, and pieces of harness equipment can be found. Unless removed by visitors, they will exist there as historic relics because of the preservation effect of the cold, dry antarctic climate. The stable roof has since blown away, but the rest of the pony shelter can be seen on the lee side of the hut. A short distance away, pony dung and a pile of horseshoe nails indicate where the animals were picketed and exercised around Pony Lake.

Looking out from under the veranda of Scott's Discovery hut

Bales of fodder used to form the outside stable wall at Scott's Cape Evans hut still remain.

MASON

D. L. HARROWFIELD, CANTERBURY MUSEUM

At Cape Evans, a few bales of fodder remain uneaten by Scott's "poor beasts," and the snowshoes that failed to help them in their trek across the ice shelf seem waiting to be used. Some of the stable boards are missing, allowing snow and ice to accumulate inside, but this is cleared periodically by New Zealand caretakers who maintain the historic sites in the area. Thanks to the New Zealanders, the blubber stove used by Oates to boil mash for the ponies appears almost as it did in 1911.

The quarters at Hut Point are probably the best preserved due to both United States and New Zealand efforts. Bits of fodder and dung, trampled in the frozen snow under the veranda, recall the ponies standing there, gazing out uncomprehendingly at the vast, barren ice shelf and the distant mountains, beyond which lay the South Pole, the magnet that drew their masters.

Bibliography

Amundsen, Roald. *The South Pole*. London: John Murray, 1912.

Cherry-Garrard, Apsley. *The Worst Journey in the World*. London: Constable, 1965.

Fisher, James and Margery. *Shackleton*. Boston: Houghton Mifflin, 1958.

Huxley, Elspeth. *Scott of the Antarctic*. New York: Atheneum, 1978.

Lashly, William. *Under Scott's Command: Lashly's Antarctic Diaries*, ed. Commander A. R. Ellis. New York: Taplinger, 1969.

Pound, Reginald. *Scott of the Antarctic*. New York: Coward-McCann, 1966.

Quartermain, L.B. *South to the Pole*. London: Oxford University Press, 1967.

Scott, Captain R.F. *Scott's Last Expedition*. New York: Dodd, Mead, 1913.

Shackleton, Ernest. *The Heart of the Antarctic*. London: Heinemann, 1909.

Wilson, E.A. *Diary of the 'Terra Nova' Expedition to the Antarctic 1910–12*, ed. H. G. R. King. London: Blandford Press, 1972.

Index

Mules (*cont'd*)
    characterized, 187, 194, 198
    compared with ponies, 195, 197–
       198
    eating habits, 187, 198
    management of, 194–195
    plans for, 135, 187, 191, 194

Nelson, Edward, 143, 161
New Zealand
    caretakers, 201
    Nimrod Expedition in, 16–23
    Terra Nova Expedition in, 97–
       102
Night marching, 123–124, 175, 195
Nimrod, 19, 32
Nimrod, 16, 18, 22–39, 75, 90
Nimrod Expedition
    at Cape Royds, 32–51
    depot-laying, 51
    in New Zealand, 16–23
    Pole trek, 54–90
    preparations for, 12–15
    voyage south, 16–31
Nobby
    coat of, 144, 158
    on depot-laying, 118, 123, 135–
      140, 145
    on Pole trek, 154, 158–163, 174,
      178–179, 182, 184
    tricks of, 158–160
Northern Party, 51, 90
North Geographic Pole, 13, 93, 98,
    185

Oates, Captain Lawrence
    character of, 122
    on depot-laying, 117, 125, 130,
      136–141
    lectures, 146, 154
    memorial to, 198
    mules, plans for, 135
    opinion of ponies, 99, 130, 173
    on Pole trek, 154, 160–177, 184,
      187, 191, 193
    pony manager, 98, 111, 118, 122,
      127, 144, 148–151
    on *Terra Nova*, 102–103, 106

Omelchenko, *see* Anton
One Ton Depot, 131, 173, 180, 191–
    194, 197, 199
Orca, *see* Killer whales
Osman, 104, 126–127, 131–133

Pack ice, 11, 22, 30, 104–106
Peary, Robert, 14, 98, 185
Polar plateau
    Amundsen crossing, 174–175, 184
    Scott crossing, 187–189
    Shackleton crossing, 81–85
Pole, *see* South Geographic Pole
Ponies. *See also* individual ponies.
    age of, 15, 69, 99–100, 198
    ailments of, 42–43, 74, 149–152
    appetite, 43, 46, 62–69, 74–78,
      137, 167, 176
    characterized, 13–14, 16
    coats of, 16, 22, 60, 106, 128, 136,
      144, 150, 154, 158, 199
    color of, 18–19, 32, 34, 95, 100
    depot-laying, used in, 117–142
    dogs, compared with, 13–14, 94,
      198–199
    evaluated, Scott, 95–96, 99–100,
      121, 131, 141, 150, 153, 156,
      160, 168, 171, 173, 184
    evaluated, Shackleton, 16–18, 52,
      94
    exercising of, 44–45, 52, 106, 117,
      144, 146–148, 156, 158
    feeding of, 14, 18–19, 22, 59, 62,
      77–78, 118, 127, 131, 146, 148,
      152, 167, 174, 176, 182, 200
    harness, 52–53, 111, 114, 162
    horses, compared with, 16, 45, 154
    intelligence of, 16, 45, 153–154
    lameness of, 54–57, 67, 100, 120,
      125
    management lectures on, 146, 154
    as meat, 13, 71–73, 75, 77, 83, 86,
      88–89, 177, 180, 187, 191
    medical examination of, 15, 22, 96
    mules, compared with, 195, 197–
      198
    on *Nimrod*, 22–32
    in northern regions, 12–14, 18–19
    picketing of, 123, 132

210

THEODORE K. MASON was born in Yreka, California, and grew up in Klamath Falls, Oregon, where he worked part-time on the city newspaper while attending high school. In 1965 he was graduated from the University of Oregon with a Bachelor of Arts degree in English.

During five years in the Navy, he was assigned as command journalist at the Naval Schools of Photography in Pensacola, Florida, and then as Armed Forces television station supervisor at Guantanamo Bay, Cuba.

He made the first of five trips to Antarctica as a journalist with the Navy's Antarctic Support Force and was based at McMurdo Station where he spent one austral summer. Later he was transferred to the "Operation Deep Freeze" advance headquarters in Christchurch, New Zealand.

Following his discharge, he taught in high school and worked as a public relations executive in Australia where his first book on the Antarctic was published. He now lives in New York City.